Fantastic once-a-week Workouts from CGP!

There are plenty of vital maths skills for pupils to learn in Year 2, that's for sure. That's why this CGP book is so handy — it's perfect for making sure all that new knowledge is sinking in.

It contains 10-Minute Maths Workouts for every week of the year, each covering a mixture of topics and skills. They're ideal to use as starter activities, recaps, homework tasks... and more!

All the answers are included, and there's even a progress chart to keep track of their scores. Trust CGP to think of everything!

Published by CGP
ISBN: 978 1 78908 312 5

Editors: Liam Dyer and Sammy El-Bahrawy
Reviewer: Lucy Towle

With thanks to Shaun Harrogate and Clare Selway for the proofreading.

Contents pages contain public sector information licensed under the Open Government Licence v3.0.
http://www.nationalarchives.gov.uk/doc/open-government-licence/version/3/

With thanks to iStock.com for permission to reproduce the photographs used
on pages 7, 15, 22, 23, 24, 25, 26, 31, 37, 49, 61, 62, 75, 77, 78, 79 and 83.
Images throughout the book from www.edu-clips.com.
Clipart from Corel®

Printed by Elanders Ltd, Newcastle upon Tyne.
Based on the classic CGP style created by Richard Parsons.

Text, design, layout and original illustrations
© Coordination Group Publications Ltd. (CGP) 2019
All rights reserved.

**Photocopying this book is not permitted, even if you have a CLA licence.
Extra copies are available from CGP with next day delivery • 0800 1712 712 • www.cgpbooks.co.uk**

How to Use this Book

- This book contains 36 workouts. We've split them into 3 sections — one for each term, with 12 workouts each. There's roughly one workout for every week of the school year.

- Each workout is out of 12 marks and should take about 10 minutes to complete.

- Each workout starts with some warm-up questions covering the number topics and ends with a problem solving question.

- The first 3 workouts only contain Year 1 Maths — they're ideal for reminding pupils what they learnt in the previous year. These workouts should be done at the start of Year 2.

- The last 9 workouts only contain Year 2 Maths — they're perfect for ensuring that pupils have got to grips with the Year 2 topics.

- The other workouts increase in difficulty as you go through the book. They contain a mix of topics from Year 1 and Year 2.

- Answers and a Progress Chart can be found at the back of the book.

The contents pages show you where each Year 2 topic is first introduced.

In each term, the new topics are only tested in the workout they're listed under on the contents page. These topics are then retested in the following terms.

This means the workouts in each term can be done in any order — pick the workout which best suits the needs of your class.

The tick boxes on the contents pages can help you to keep a record of which workouts have been attempted.

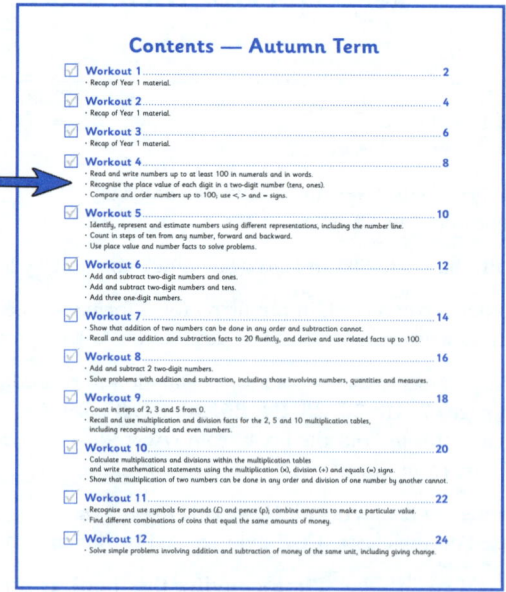

Contents — Autumn Term

☑ **Workout 1** 2
 • Recap of Year 1 material.

☑ **Workout 2** 4
 • Recap of Year 1 material.

☑ **Workout 3** 6
 • Recap of Year 1 material.

☑ **Workout 4** 8
 • Read and write numbers up to at least 100 in numerals and in words.
 • Recognise the place value of each digit in a two-digit number (tens, ones).
 • Compare and order numbers up to 100; use <, > and = signs.

☑ **Workout 5** 10
 • Identify, represent and estimate numbers using different representations, including the number line.
 • Count in steps of ten from any number, forward and backward.
 • Use place value and number facts to solve problems.

☑ **Workout 6** 12
 • Add and subtract two-digit numbers and ones.
 • Add and subtract two-digit numbers and tens.
 • Add three one-digit numbers.

☑ **Workout 7** 14
 • Show that addition of two numbers can be done in any order and subtraction cannot.
 • Recall and use addition and subtraction facts to 20 fluently, and derive and use related facts up to 100.

☑ **Workout 8** 16
 • Add and subtract 2 two-digit numbers.
 • Solve problems with addition and subtraction, including those involving numbers, quantities and measures.

☑ **Workout 9** 18
 • Count in steps of 2, 3 and 5 from 0.
 • Recall and use multiplication and division facts for the 2, 5 and 10 multiplication tables, including recognising odd and even numbers.

☑ **Workout 10** 20
 • Calculate multiplications and divisions within the multiplication tables and write mathematical statements using the multiplication (×), division (÷) and equals (=) signs.
 • Show that multiplication of two numbers can be done in any order and division of one number by another cannot.

☑ **Workout 11** 22
 • Recognise and use symbols for pounds (£) and pence (p); combine amounts to make a particular value.
 • Find different combinations of coins that equal the same amounts of money.

☑ **Workout 12** 24
 • Solve simple problems involving addition and subtraction of money of the same unit, including giving change.

Contents — Spring Term

☑ **Workout 1** **26**
- Solve problems with addition and subtraction using mental and written methods.
- Recognise and use the inverse relationship between addition and subtraction, and use this to check calculations and solve missing number problems.

☑ **Workout 2** **28**
- Solve problems involving multiplication and division, using materials, arrays, repeated addition, mental methods, and multiplication and division facts, including problems in contexts.

☑ **Workout 3** **30**
- Choose and use appropriate units to estimate and measure length/height (m/cm), using rulers.
- Compare and order length, and record the results using >, < and =.

☑ **Workout 4** **32**
- Choose and use appropriate units to estimate and measure mass (kg/g), using scales.
- Compare and order mass, and record the results using >, < and =.

☑ **Workout 5** **34**
- Choose and use appropriate units to estimate and measure volume/capacity (litres/ml), using measuring vessels.
- Compare and order volume/capacity and record the results using >, < and =.

☑ **Workout 6** **36**
- Identify and describe the properties of 2D shapes, including the number of sides and symmetry in a vertical line.
- Compare and sort common 2D shapes and everyday objects.

☑ **Workout 7** **38**
- Identify and describe the properties of 3D shapes, including the number of edges, vertices and faces.
- Identify 2D shapes on the surface of 3D shapes.
- Compare and sort common 3D shapes and everyday objects.

☑ **Workout 8** **40**
- Interpret and construct tally charts and simple tables.
- Count, total, compare and sort categorical data in tally charts and tables.

☑ **Workout 9** **42**
- Interpret and construct simple pictograms.
- Count, total, compare and sort categorical data in pictograms.

☑ **Workout 10** **44**
- Interpret and construct block diagrams.
- Count, total, compare and sort categorical data in block diagrams.

☑ **Workout 11** **46**
- Estimate and measure temperature (°C), using thermometers.
- Tell and write the time to five minutes, including quarter past and quarter to the hour and draw the hands on a clock face to show these times.

☑ **Workout 12** **48**
- Know the number of minutes in an hour and the number of hours in a day.
- Compare and sequence intervals of time.

Contents — Summer Term

☑ **Workout 1** 50
- Recognise, find and name $\frac{1}{2}$ and $\frac{1}{3}$ of a length, shape, set of objects or quantity.
- Write simple fractions of amounts.

☑ **Workout 2** 52
- Recognise, find and name $\frac{1}{4}$ and $\frac{3}{4}$ of a length, shape, set of objects or quantity.
- Recognise the equivalence of $\frac{2}{4}$ and $\frac{1}{2}$.

☑ **Workout 3** 54
- Order and arrange combinations of mathematical objects in patterns and sequences.
- Use mathematical vocabulary to describe position, direction and movement, including movement in a straight line and distinguishing between rotation as a turn and in terms of right angles for quarter, half and three-quarter turns (clockwise and anticlockwise).

☑ **Workout 4** 56
- Recap of Year 2 material.

☑ **Workout 5** 58
- Recap of Year 2 material.

☑ **Workout 6** 60
- Recap of Year 2 material.

☑ **Workout 7** 62
- Recap of Year 2 material.

☑ **Workout 8** 64
- Recap of Year 2 material.

☑ **Workout 9** 66
- Recap of Year 2 material.

☑ **Workout 10** 68
- Recap of Year 2 material.

☑ **Workout 11** 70
- Recap of Year 2 material.

☑ **Workout 12** 72
- Recap of Year 2 material.

Progress Chart 74

Answers 75

Autumn Term: Workout 1

Warm up

1. Circle the tower with the **most windows**.

   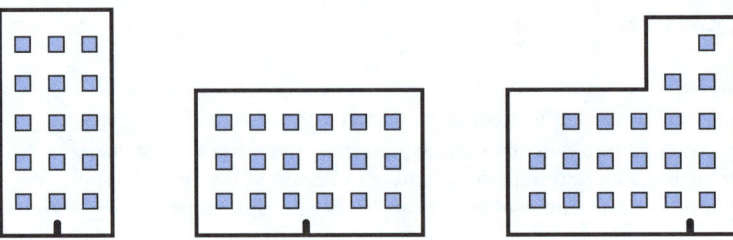

   1 mark

2. Write each number as a **word**.

   12 ....   17 ....

   2 marks

3. Circle the **heavier bird**.

   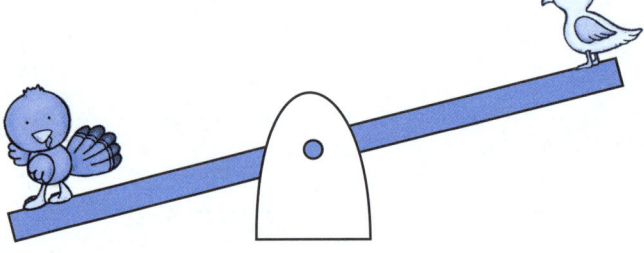

   1 mark

4. Work out these **multiplications**.

   4 × 2 = ...

   1 mark

   3 × 5 = ...

   1 mark

5. **Tick (✓)** the **tallest** object.

giraffe ☐ candle ☐ doll ☐

1 mark

6. Write the **time** shown on this clock.

....

1 mark

7. Work out:

6 add 12 equals ....

1 mark

18 subtract 7 equals ....

1 mark

8. Sarah stands on the **cross** below facing **star 2**.

   Tick (✓) the **turns** she could make to face **star 1**.

   a quarter turn anticlockwise ☐
   a half turn anticlockwise ☐
   a three-quarter turn clockwise ☐
   a quarter turn clockwise ☐

2 marks

Score: ☐

Autumn Term: Workout 2

Warm up

1. Fill in the **missing number**.

   1 mark

2. Write **+** or **−** in each box.

   3 ☐ 4 = 7   4 = 5 ☐ 1

   10 ☐ 8 = 2   9 = 4 ☐ 5

   1 mark

   1 mark

3. Match each **shape** to the **right description**.

   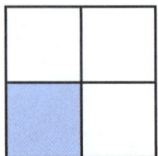 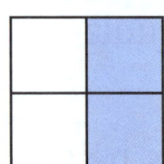 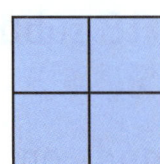

   | one whole is shaded | one half is shaded | one quarter is shaded |

   2 marks

4. Circle the **longest time**.

   10 hours   15 hours   1 hour

   1 mark

5. Look at the stack of **shapes**.

   Name the shape at the **top**.

   ....
   1 mark

   Name the shape at the **bottom**.

   ....
   1 mark

6. Work out:

   14 add 6 equals ....
   1 mark

   19 subtract 3 equals ....
   1 mark

7. Share **15** pencils **equally** between **5** children.

   Each child gets .... pencils.
   1 mark

8. Look at this **pattern** of numbers.

1st	2nd	3rd	4th	5th	6th	7th
100	99	98	97			

   What is the **7th** number in the pattern? ....
   1 mark

   Score:

Autumn Term: Workout 3

Warm up

1. Circle the number that is **more than 15**.

    14   11   16   9

    1 mark

2. Match each **sum** to the **right answer**.

    | 0 add 10 | — | 10 |
    | 15 add 2 | | 20 |
    | 12 add 8 | | 17 |
    | 2 add 12 | | 14 |

    2 marks

3. Match each **picture** to the **right words**.

       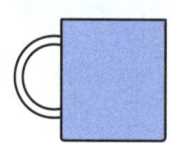   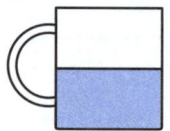   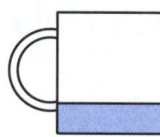

    half full   quarter full   full

    2 marks

4. Fill in the **missing numbers**.

    .... + 3 = 15   3 = ... − 8

    2 marks

5. If today is **Sunday**, what day was **yesterday**?

   ....

   1 mark

6. Count up in steps of **ten** from **0** to **50**.
   Cross (**X**) **two** numbers you **do not** say.

   10   15   20   25   30
   ☐   ☐   ☐   ☐   ☐

   1 mark

7. Circle **two** coins that have a value of **more than 10p**.

   2 marks

8. Niall puts **2 flags** in every **sandcastle** he builds.

   He builds **7 sandcastles**.
   How many **flags** does he need?

   .... flags

   1 mark

   Score: ☐

Autumn Term: Workout 3

Autumn Term: Workout 4

Warm up

1. **Tick** (✓) the sentence that is **right**.

   99 is one more than 100 ☐

   101 is one more than 100 ☐

   1 mark

2. **Add 4** to each number.

   8 ....   14 ....

   2 marks

3. **Fill in** the gaps in this sentence.

   65 has a .... in the tens place

   and a .... in the ones place.

   1 mark

4. Colour in **half** of these shapes.

   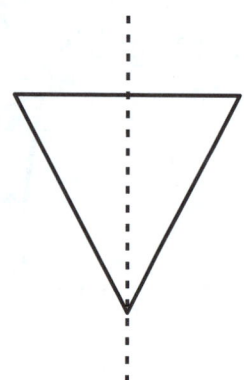   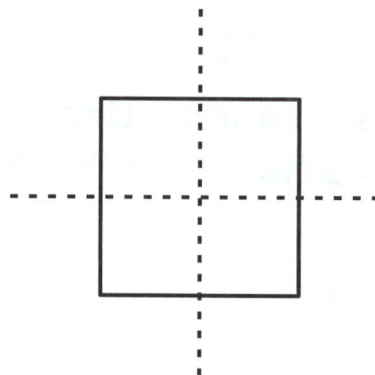

   2 marks

5. **Tick (✓) the lightest animal.**

   6 kg 10 kg 2 kg
   ☐ ☐ ☐

   1 mark

6. Look at the **numbers** in this box. | 78 76 96 |

   What is the largest number? ....
   1 mark

   Write the smallest number in words.

   ....
   1 mark

7. Write **<, >** or **=** in each box.

   70 ☐ 47   22 ☐ 29

   2 marks

8. Jon says, "**One hour ago**, both hands on this clock pointed to **12**."

   Draw hands on the clock to show the time **now**.

   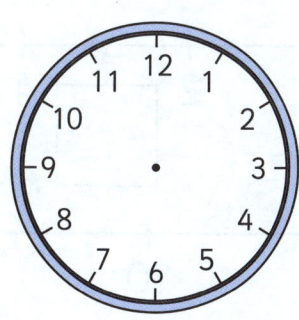

   1 mark

   Score:

Autumn Term: Workout 5

Warm up

1. Work out **one less** than **20**.

   ....
   1 mark

2. Put **+**, **−** or **=** in the boxes.

   1 ☐ 5 ☐ 4   7 ☐ 3 ☐ 10

   2 marks

3. How much **water** is in the bottle? Write **millilitres** or **litres** in your answer.

   ....
   1 mark

4. **Estimate** the numbers the **arrows** are pointing to.

   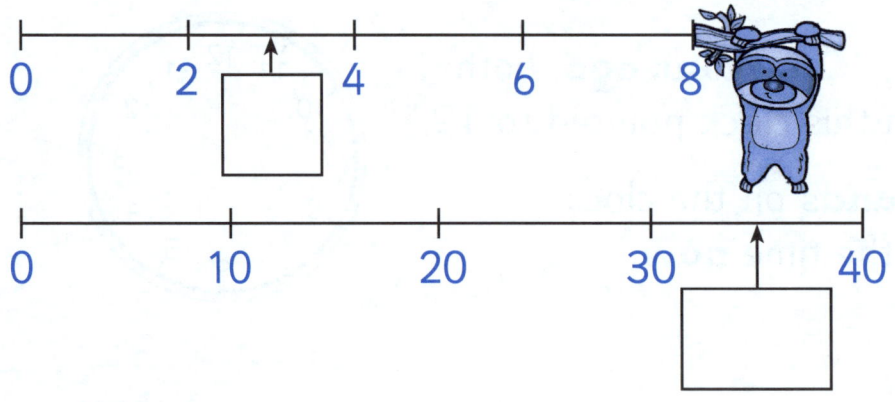

   1 mark

   1 mark

5. Count up in steps of **ten** to fill in the missing number.

      17   27   37   ....

1 mark

6. Share **10** pennies into **2 equal** piles to help fill in the missing number.

    10 ÷ 2 = ...

1 mark

7. These shapes make the number **24**. Each shape represents a **ten** or a **one**.

    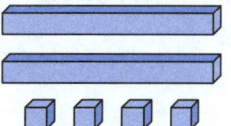

    Find the **missing numbers** made by these shapes.

    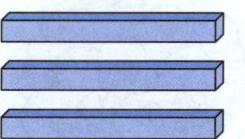   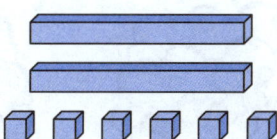

    ....

2 marks

8. Ellie **adds** a number to itself. The sum equals **one more** than **15**.

    Fill in the **gaps** to show her sum.

       .... + ... = ...

2 marks

Score:

Autumn Term: Workout 6

Warm up

1. Write the sentence using **numbers** and **signs**.

   Twelve subtract two equals ten. ....

   1 mark

2. Complete these **multiplications**.

   $6 \times 2 = $ ....

   1 mark

   $4 \times 5 = $ ....

   1 mark

3. Look at the picture.

   Circle the monkey **behind** a **tree**.

   1 mark

4. Fill in the **missing total**.

   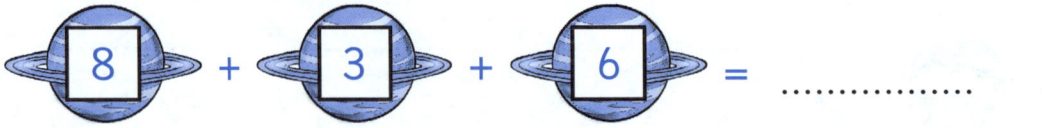

   1 mark

5. Fill in the **missing number**.

   There are .... days in a week.

   1 mark

6. Work out:

   31 + 8 = ...   52 + 20 = ...

   2 marks

   48 − 6 = ...   97 − 30 = ...

   2 marks

7. Circle the tower that is **half as tall** as the tower in the box.

   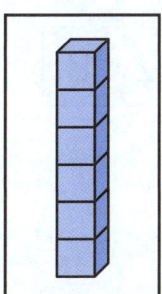 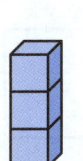 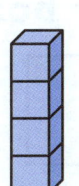 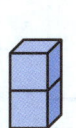 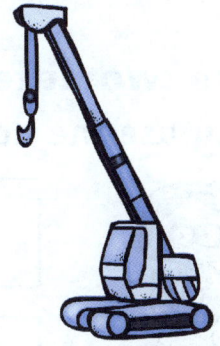

   1 mark

8. Look at this **pattern**.

   Which number would be in the **next circle**?

   ....

   1 mark

   Score:

Autumn Term: Workout 7

Warm up

1. Draw **more raindrops** (💧) so there are **16** in total.

   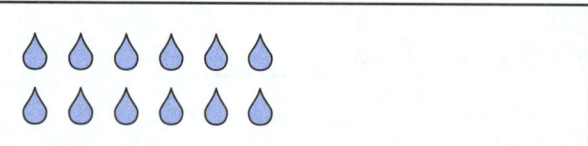

   1 mark

2. Work out the **answers**.

   3 + 8 = ...   14 − 7 = ...

   2 marks

3. Make **two different** number sentences. **Only** use the numbers in the **box**.

   ☐ + ☐ = ☐

   ☐ + ☐ = ☐

   2 marks

4. Colour in **one quarter** of this shape.

   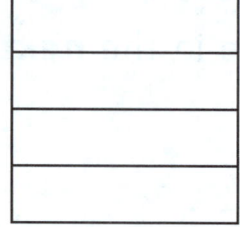

   1 mark

5. These clocks show times in the **afternoon**.
   Circle the clock that shows the **earlier time**.

   1 mark

6. Fill in the **missing numbers**.

   .... + 70 = 100   20 + ... = 100

   2 marks

7. Find the **total amount** in each box.

   .... p   .... p

   2 marks

8. Finley has a glass of juice.
   It is **more** than a **quarter full**
   and **less** than **half full**.

   Which glass is his?
   Circle **A**, **B** or **C**.

   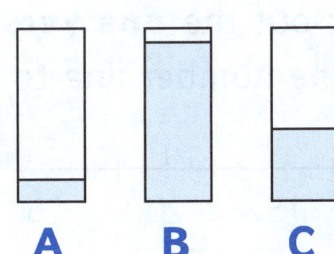

   A   B   C

   1 mark

   Score:

Autumn Term: Workout 8

Warm up

1. Count backwards in steps of **two** from **8**.

   8 2

   1 mark

2. **Draw dots** to make each number sentence **right**.

   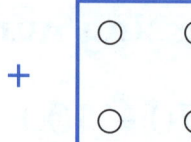

   2 marks

3. **Fill in** the gap below.

   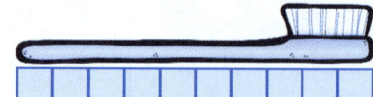

   The toothbrush is .... blocks long.

   1 mark

4. Work out the **answers** below.
   Use the number line to help you.

   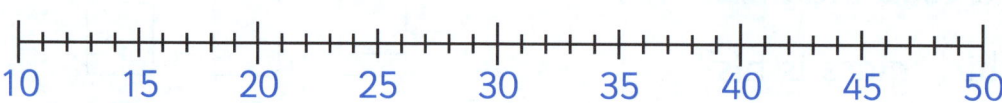

   14 + 23 = ...   38 − 16 = ...

   2 marks

5. Draw **hands** on each clock to show the **right time**.

   4 o'clock   half past 10

   2 marks

6. Work out the **answers**.

   27 + 12   66 − 34

   ....
   2 marks

7. Fill in the **boxes** to find the **total** number of crayons.

   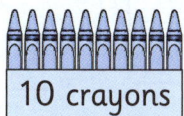

   3 × ☐ = ☐
   1 mark

8. Rosa has a packet of **25** seeds.
   She uses **13** seeds.

   How many seeds are **left**?

   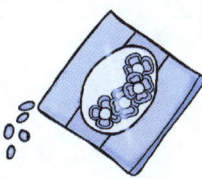

   .... seeds
   1 mark

   Score:

Autumn Term: Workout 9

Warm up

1. Write **twenty** as a **number**.

   ....
   1 mark

2. Write the **number** you reach each time.

   Start at 10. Count up five. .... 1 mark

   Start at 8. Count up ten. .... 1 mark

3. Fill in the **missing numbers**.

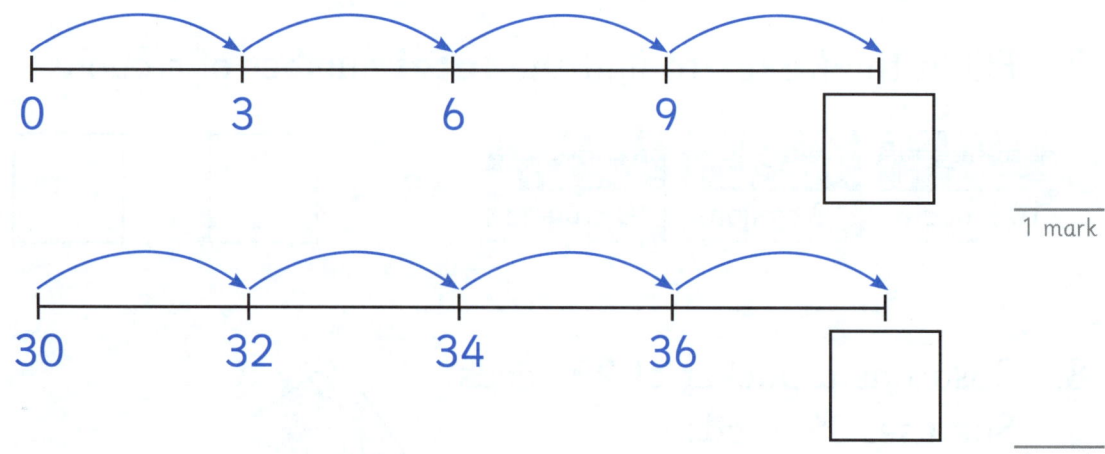

   1 mark

   1 mark

4. Circle the **two even** numbers.

   7   22   31   34   43

   2 marks

5. **Tick** (✓) the box where the arrow points **after** a **whole turn**.

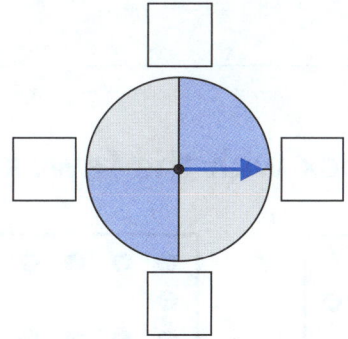

1 mark

6. Circle the **correct word** to complete the sentence.

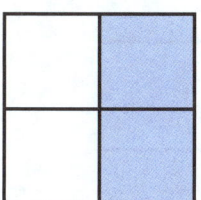

One quarter / half / whole of the shape is shaded.

1 mark

7. Fill in the **missing numbers**.

2 × 10 = ... ÷ 5 = 5

2 marks

8. Vera throws some snowballs.

Her first throw was **19 m long**.
Her second throw was **1 m shorter**.

How far was her **second throw**?

.... m

1 mark

Score:

Autumn Term: Workout 10

Warm up

1. Circle the box with the **fewest dots**.

   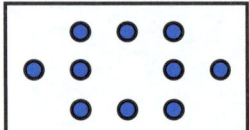 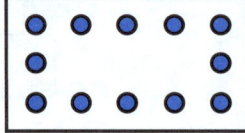 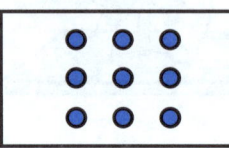

   1 mark

2. Fill in the **missing numbers** in the boxes.

   2 marks

3. Count backwards in **steps of ten** from **50**.
   Write the **next four** numbers you reach.

   50   ....

   2 marks

4. Circle **3 equal** groups of turtles.

   1 mark

   Use your groups to write a **division** number sentence.

   ....

   1 mark

5. Fill in the **missing number**.

   6 × 10 = 10 × ....

   1 mark

6. Look at the objects on the shelf.

   Circle the **pyramid**.

   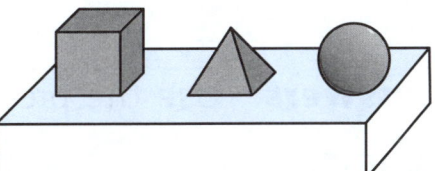

   1 mark

7. Write **×**, **÷** or **=** in each box.

   4 ☐ 5 ☐ 20   6 ☐ 30 ☐ 5

   2 marks

8. 3 friends **finished** a race. Here are their times.

Amir	50 seconds
Jordan	40 seconds
Rita	45 seconds

   Who **won** the race? ....

   1 mark

   Score: ☐

Autumn Term: Workout 11

Warm up

1. Circle the number **one more** than **19**.

   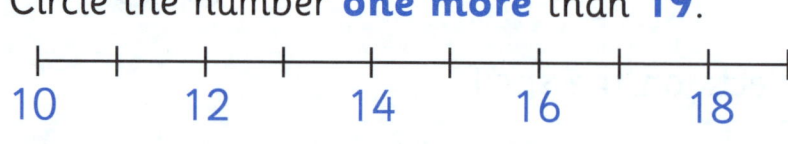

   1 mark

2. Fill in the **answers**. Use the pictures to help you.

   ○○○○ ○○○○ $8 \div 2 = $ ....

   1 mark

   ○○ ○○ ○○ ○○ ○○ $10 \div 5 = $ ....

   1 mark

3. Look at the coin on the right.

   Circle **two** amounts with the **same value** as the coin.

   1p   100p   10p   £1   £10

   2 marks

4. Use the ruler to draw a **cross** on the line **5 cm** from **point A**.

   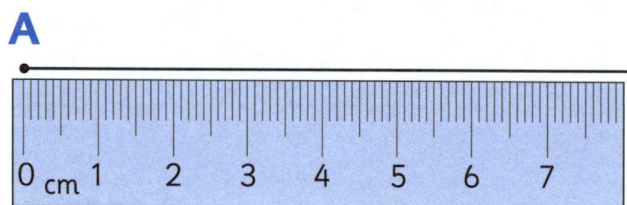

   1 mark

5. Circle **two coins** that add to **make 12p**.

    1 mark

    Circle **three coins** that add to **make 12p**.

    1 mark

6. Match each **subtraction** to its **missing number**.

    | ☐ − 7 = 13 | | 0 |
    | 20 − ☐ = 20 | | 10 |
    | 20 − ☐ = 10 | | 19 |
    | 20 − 1 = ☐ | | 20 |

    3 marks

7. Gabby cuts a pie into **four equal** slices.
    She eats **three** slices.

    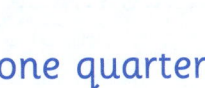

    Circle the amount of pie that is **left**.

    one quarter   one half   three quarters

    1 mark

    Score:

Autumn Term: Workout 12

Warm up

1. Fill in the **missing numbers**.

   0   2   4   ....

     5   10   15   ....

2. **Subtract 3** from each number.

   16 ....   20 ....

3. A pencil costs **15p**. Yuri pays with a **20p** coin. **Tick** (✓) the coin he gets as **change**.

   ☐   ☐   ☐

4. Work out these **multiplications**.

   6 × 2 = ...

   4 × 5 = ...

5. Look at these items.

muffin 40p   cookie 25p

How much do a muffin and a cookie cost in **total**?

.... p   *1 mark*

How much **more** does a muffin cost than a cookie?

.... p   *1 mark*

6. Layla buys an ice cream for **50p**.
   She uses **3 coins** and gets **no change**.

   Circle the **coins** she pays with.

   2 marks

7. Felix describes when his **birthday** is.

   > **Yesterday** was **Tuesday**.
   > My birthday is **tomorrow**.

   Fill in the missing **day of the week**.

   Felix's birthday is on ....

   1 mark

   Score:

Spring Term: Workout 1

Warm up

1. Fill in the **missing numbers**.

    57   58   61   ....

    2 marks

2. Circle **all** of the **odd numbers** below.

    6   9   15   18   22   28   50   57

    2 marks

3. **Add up** each group of **coins**.

    .... p   .... p

    2 marks

4. Hans has worked out this **subtraction**.

    Which **addition** could he do to **check** his answer? **Tick** (✓) the box.

    88 + 9 ☐   79 + 9 ☐   79 + 88 ☐

    1 mark

5. Fill in the **missing number**.

    .... − 75 = 11

1 mark

6. Draw **one line** on the rectangle below to **split** it into **two rectangles**.

1 mark

Draw **one line** on the rectangle below to **split** it into **two triangles**.

1 mark

7. Colette has **15 bananas**.
Sanjay has **20 bananas**.

They eat **4 bananas**.

How many bananas are **left**?

.... bananas

2 marks

Score:

Spring Term: Workout 2

Warm up

1. Fill in the **missing numbers**.

    40 + 20 = ...

    1 mark

    55 − 30 = ...

    1 mark

2. Write the numbers the **arrows** are pointing to.

2 marks

3. What **3D shape** is this ball?

....

1 mark

4. There are **10 cows** in a field.

    Each cow has **4 legs**.

    How many **legs** are there in **total**?

.... legs

1 mark

5. Nora says, "If I **multiply** my age by **5**, I get **35**."

   How old is Nora?

   .... years old

   1 mark

6. Emil works out the following **sum**.

   2 + 2 + 2 + 2 + 2 + 2 = 12

   Write down a **multiplication fact** using Emil's sum.

   ☐ × 2 = ☐

   1 mark

7. The box below shows some **days of the week**. Write down the days that are **missing**.

   | Monday |
   | Tuesday |
   | Thursday |
   | Sunday |

   ....

   ....

   ....

   2 marks

8. Jasmine is thinking of a **two-digit number**.

   She says, "The ones digit is an **even number**. The tens digit is **three times** the ones digit."

   What is **Jasmine's number**?

   ....

   2 marks

   Score: ☐

Spring Term: Workout 3

Warm up

1. Write these numbers in **words**.

    19 ....

    11 ....

    2 marks

2. Count in **steps of ten** to fill in the **missing numbers**.

    87   77   47

    1 mark

3. Colour in **half** of these shapes.

    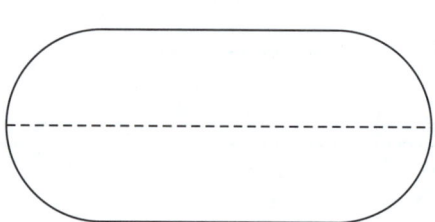   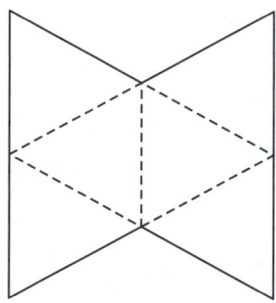

    2 marks

4. **Tick** (✓) the **best unit** for measuring the **length** of:

       a train   cm ☐   m ☐

    1 mark

       a carrot   cm ☐   m ☐

    1 mark

5. Circle all the **even numbers** in the **5 times table**.

   2   5   8   10   15
   16   20   22   25   30

   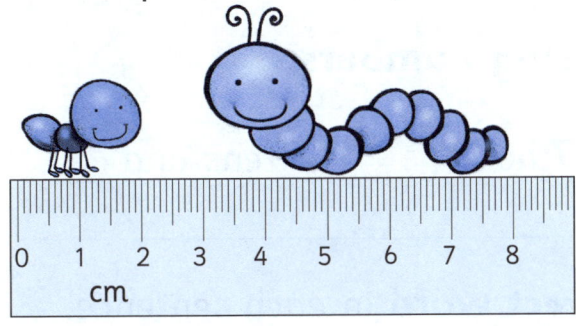

   2 marks

6. An ant and a caterpillar were measured with a **ruler**.

   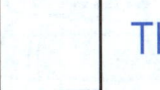

   Write **<**, **>** or **=** in the box.

   The ant's length ☐ The caterpillar's length

   1 mark

7. Draw **two more coins** in the **box** on the **right** so both boxes have the **same amount** of money.

      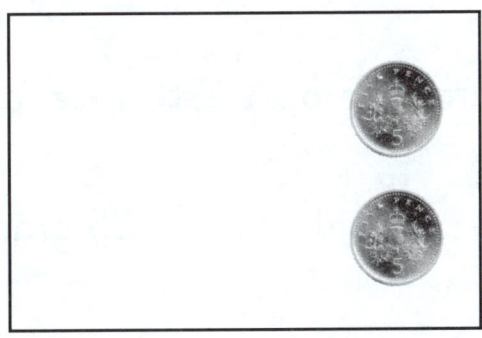

   2 marks

   Score:

Spring Term: Workout 4

Warm up

1. Work out these **additions**.

    11 + 3 = ...   8 + 9 = ...

    2 marks

2. Fill in the **missing numbers**.

    The number **37** has .... tens and .... ones.

    1 mark

3. Circle the **correct word** in each sentence.

    The reading book is the   top / middle / bottom   book.

    1 mark

    The maths book is the   top / middle / bottom   book.

    1 mark

4. Circle the **best estimate** for the **weight** of:

    a child   25 grams   25 kilograms

    1 mark

    a pencil   10 grams   10 kilograms

    1 mark

5. Circle **all** of the **multiplications** that equal **20**.

   2 × 5   10 × 10   4 × 5

   10 × 2   5 × 2   4 × 10   4 × 2

   5 × 10   2 × 10   12 × 5

   2 marks

6. Gus weighs an **egg** on these scales.

   Tick (✓) the correct sentence.

   The mass of the egg < 45 grams ☐
   The mass of the egg = 45 grams ☐
   The mass of the egg > 45 grams ☐

   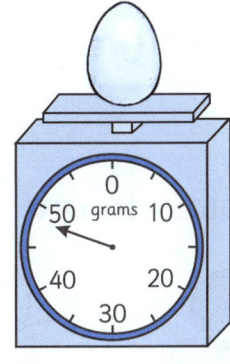

   1 mark

7. Three children are playing a game.

   Alya has **6 points**.
   Jayden has **2 more points** than Alya.
   Maybelle has **3 points**.

   How many **points** do they have **altogether**?

   .... points

   2 marks

   Score: ☐

Spring Term: Workout 5

Warm up

1. Count in **steps of five** to fill in the **missing number**.

    5   10   15   25

    1 mark

2. Work out these **calculations**.

    42 + 10 = ...   77 − 60 = ...

    2 marks

3. Colour in **one quarter** of these shapes.

  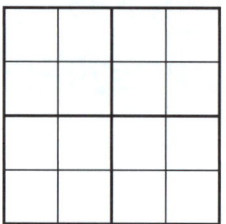

2 marks

4. **Cross out** (**X**) **two** calculations that are **wrong**.

    4 × 5 = 20   20 ÷ 5 = 4   4 ÷ 20 = 5

    5 ÷ 20 = 4   5 × 4 = 20   20 ÷ 4 = 5

2 marks

5. Write **<**, **>** or **=** in the box.

    10 ml  1 litre

    1 mark

6. These **4 jugs** hold different amounts of water.

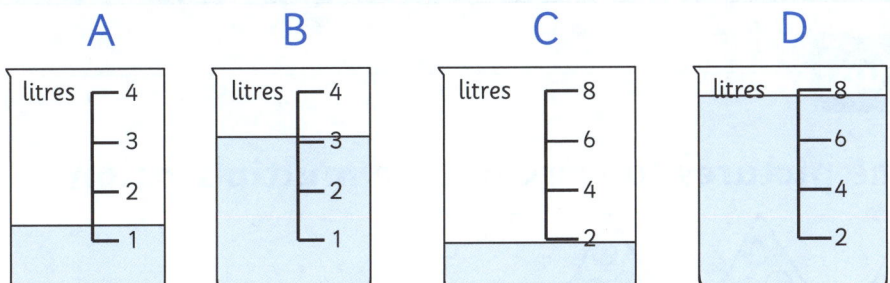

Put the **letters** of the jugs in **order**.
Start with the jug holding the **most water**.

....
most water   least water

2 marks

Which **jug** contains about **2 litres**?

Jug ....

1 mark

7. Ronnie always goes to **Maths Club**.

Maths Club

Every Monday, Wednesday and Friday

Ronnie says, "I went to Maths Club **yesterday**, but Maths Club isn't on **tomorrow**."

Which **day of the week** is it?

....

1 mark

Score:

Spring Term: Workout 6

Warm up

1. Use the **pictures** to work out the **multiplication**.

        3 × 6 = ...

   1 mark

2. Work out these **subtractions**.

   58 − 4 = ...   81 − 10 = ...

   2 marks

3. How many **sides** does a **pentagon** have?
   Circle your answer.

   3   4   5   6   7   8

   1 mark

4. Sort these **shapes** into the correct part of the **table**.
   One has been done for you.

     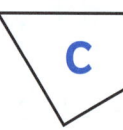  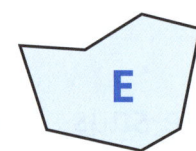

Has 6 sides	Does not have 6 sides
	A

   2 marks

5. Work out these **additions**.

   34 + 55 = ...   48 + 34 = ...

   2 marks

6. Draw a **line of symmetry** on this **rectangle**.

   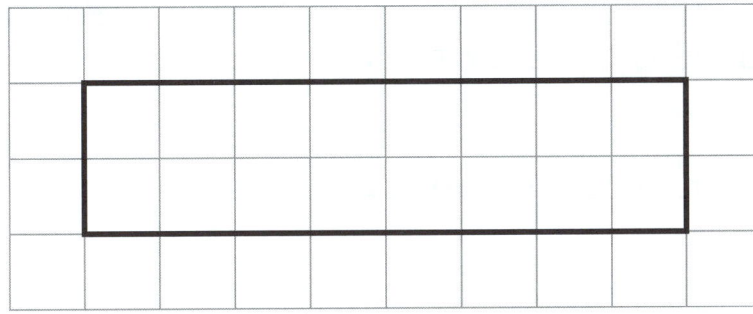 

   1 mark

7. Circle **three coins** to make a total of **24p**.

   1 mark

8. Abbie and Kaine **count up** from **0**.

   Abbie counts in steps of **5**.
   Kaine counts in steps of **3**.

   What is the **first** number after 0 that they **both** say?

   .... 2 marks

   Score:

Spring Term: Workout 7

Warm up

1. There are **12 lions**, **14 tigers** and **11 giraffes** in a zoo.

   Which animal is there **most** of?

   ....

   1 mark

2. Write these numbers in **words**.

   26 ....

   1 mark

   73 ....

   1 mark

3. Circle the **3D shape** that has the **fewest vertices**.

   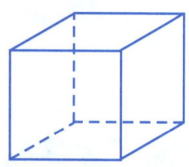   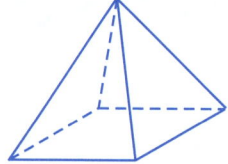   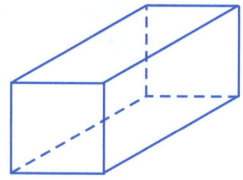

   1 mark

4. Draw **hands** on this **clock face** to show **half past 11**.

   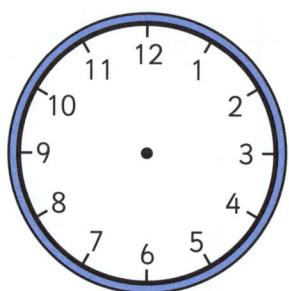

   1 mark

5. Put these numbers **in order**. Start with the **largest**.

   34   41   48   32

   ....
   largest   smallest

   2 marks

6. This shape is a **triangular prism**.

   Fill in the **missing numbers** in the table.

Faces	Edges	Vertices
	9	

   2 marks

   Tick (✓) the correct sentence.

   Four of the faces are rectangles. ☐

   Two of the faces are triangles. ☐

   1 mark

7. In a game, when you press a **button**, this arrow does a **quarter turn**.

   How many times do you need to press the button to make the arrow do **two and a half turns**?

   .... times

   2 marks

   Score:

   Spring Term: Workout 7

Spring Term: Workout 8

Warm up

1. Join up the pairs of numbers that **add up to 20**.

6   12   14

11   8   9

2 marks

2. Count in **steps of three** to fill in the **missing numbers**.

    15   ……….   ……….   ……….   27

2 marks

3. Colour all the **triangles** in the picture below.

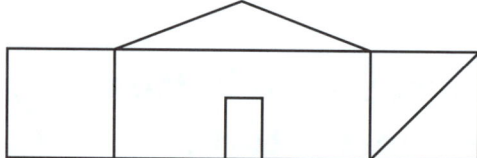

1 mark

4. Write the **missing number** in the box.

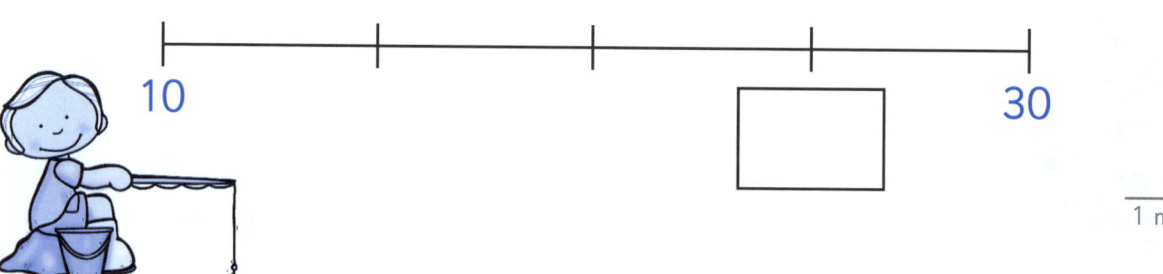

10   30

1 mark

5. Skye asked **12** people what their **first pet** was. Her results are below.

   Cat, Rock, Cat, Dog, Dog, Cat
   Rock, Cat, Dog, Cat, Dog, Cat

   Fill in the **tally chart** below to show Skye's results.

Pet	Cat	Dog	Rock
Tally			

   2 marks

   Which pet was the **most popular**?

   .... *1 mark*

   How many **more** people said 'Dog' than 'Rock'?

   .... people *1 mark*

6. A **pumpkin** weighs **6 kilograms**.
   A **watermelon** weighs **8 kilograms**.

   Write **<, >** or **=** in the box below.
   Show your working.

   weight of 5 pumpkins ☐ weight of 3 watermelons

   2 marks

   Score: ☐

Spring Term: Workout 9

Warm up

1. Work out the **missing numbers**.

   5 + ☐ = 11   15 − ☐ = 8

   2 marks

2. Work out these **multiplications**.

   4 × 5 = ...   7 × 2 = ...

   2 marks

3. The time now is **half past 2**.

   What time was it **one hour ago**?
   Circle your answer.

   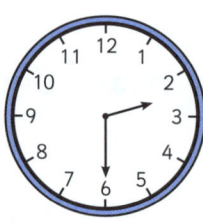

   half past 12   1 o'clock

   half past 1   2 o'clock

   1 mark

4. Ruth says, "**19 + 30** is equal to **69 − 30**."

   Is Ruth **correct**? Show your working.

   ....

   ....

   2 marks

5. Charlie records the number of **goals scored** by some **football players**. He draws a pictogram to show the results.

Player	Number of Goals
Alana	○○○
Briony	○○
Caleb	○○○○○
David	

Key:
○ = 1 goal

David scored **2 goals**. Complete the pictogram.

1 mark

Who scored the **most** goals?

....

1 mark

How many goals were scored **in total**?

.... goals

1 mark

6. Wyatt has **75p** in his pocket.

Which **coins** would he have if he has:

three coins?   ....p, ...p and ....p

1 mark

four coins?   ....p, ...p, ...p and ....p

1 mark

Score:

Spring Term: Workout 10

Warm up

1. Count in **steps of two** to fill in the **missing numbers**.

    16   10   8   ....

    2 marks

2. Work out:

    7 + 3 + 2 = ...   *1 mark*

    6 + 4 + 8 = ...   *1 mark*

3. Circle the **arrow** that points to the **left** of the turtle.

    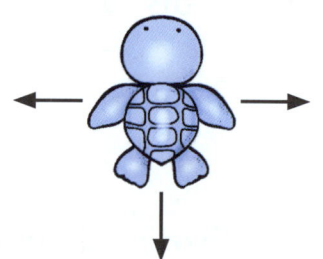

    1 mark

4. **Tick (✓)** the **two** sentences that are **correct**.

    8 + 2 is the same as 2 + 8 ☐

    8 − 2 is the same as 2 − 8 ☐

    8 × 2 is the same as 2 × 8 ☐

    8 ÷ 2 is the same as 2 ÷ 8 ☐

    2 marks

5. Tina's Bakery sells **loaves**, **rolls** and **cakes**. Tina draws a **block diagram** to show **how many** of each she sold today.

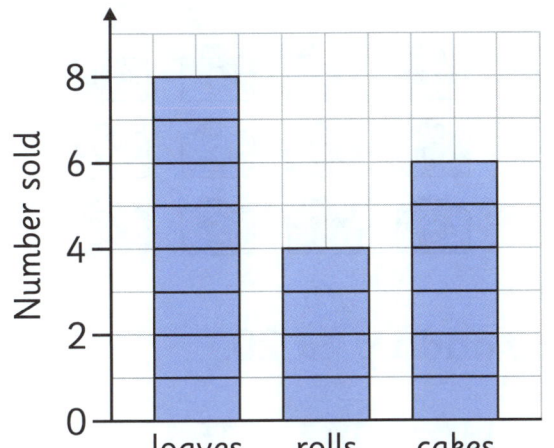

How many of each did she sell?

.... loaves

.... rolls

.... cakes

2 marks

Each roll costs **10p**. How much did people spend on **rolls** today?

.... p

1 mark

6. Use the **number cards** below to make **two different calculations** that add up to **97**.

2 marks

Spring Term: Workout 11

Warm up

1. Use the **pictures** to work out:

    12 ÷ 4 = ...

    1 mark

    12 ÷ 3 = ...

    1 mark

2. Circle the **two numbers** that **add up to 20**.

    3   4   6   7   11   14   15   19

    1 mark

3. Work out these **additions**.

    36 + 11 = ...   25 + 25 = ...

    2 marks

4. Draw the **hands** on the **clock faces** to show the right **times**.

    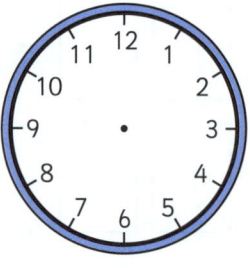   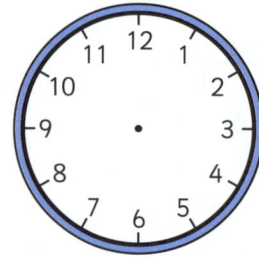

    twenty past ten   five to three

    2 marks

Spring Term: Workout 11

5. These **thermometers** show the **temperature**, in **°C**, in four different **countries**.

Iceland   Egypt   Italy   UK

The temperature in the **UK** is **8 °C**.
Draw this on the **thermometer**.

1 mark

What is the **temperature** in the **hottest** country?

.... °C

1 mark

How much **warmer** is it in **Italy** than the **UK**?

.... °C

1 mark

6. A shop sells apples in **bags of 3** or **boxes of 5**.

Flora buys **seven bags** of apples.
Monty buys **four boxes** of apples.

Who has **more** apples? Show your working.

....

2 marks

Score:

Spring Term: Workout 12

Warm up

1. Work out these **subtractions**.

   17 – 7 = ... 13 – 8 = ...

   2 marks

2. Write **<**, **>** or **=** in the boxes.

   21 ☐ 67   54 ☐ 54   93 ☐ 88

   2 marks

3. Circle the object that is shaped like a **cube**.

   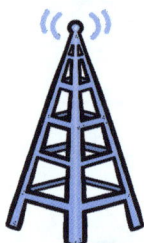  

   1 mark

4. Match each **description** to the right **number**.

Number of minutes in an hour	7
Number of hours in a day	24
Number of days in a week	60

   2 marks

5. Maisie, Dale and Zack each went for a **hot air balloon** ride.

   Maisie's ride lasted **67 minutes**.
   Dale's ride lasted **58 minutes**.
   Zack's ride lasted **1 hour**.

   Whose ride lasted the **longest**? **Circle** your answer.

   Maisie   Dale   Zack

   1 mark

6. Write **×** or **÷** in each box.

   6 ☐ 2 = 3   9 ☐ 2 = 18

   1 mark

7. Fill in the **missing number**.

   24 + 3 = 30 − ....

   1 mark

8. Saffron has **3 different coins**.

   Each coin is worth **less than £1**.
   Two coins are shaped like **circles**.

   What is the **largest** amount of money she could have?

   .... p

   2 marks

   Score: ☐

Summer Term: Workout 1

Warm up

1. Fill in the **missing number**.

   The number .... has 7 tens and 2 ones.

   1 mark

2. Work out these **additions**.

   83 + 5 = ...   48 + 7 = ...

   2 marks

3. **Colour in** $\frac{1}{3}$ of this shape.

   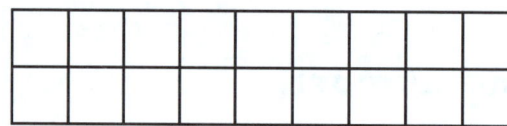

   1 mark

   Use your answer to find $\frac{1}{3}$ **of 18**.

   ....

   1 mark

4. Penny weighs a **pencil** and a **sharpener**.

   The pencil weighs **45 grams**.
   The sharpener weighs **50 grams**.

   Put **<**, **>** or **=** in the box.

   Weight of the pencil ☐ Weight of the sharpener

   1 mark

5. Circle **two shapes** that could be **faces** of a **cuboid**.

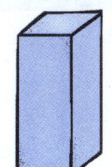
circle   rectangle   cube   triangle

pyramid   square   sphere

2 marks

6. Fill in the **missing fractions**.

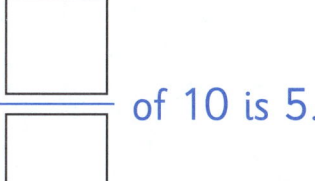 of 10 is 5.

1 mark

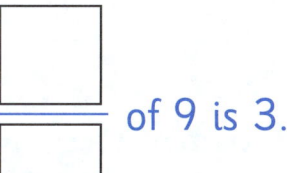 of 9 is 3.

1 mark

7. Kyle had **30 apples**.

He **gave 8 away** to his friends and fed some to his **horse**.

Kyle has **19 apples** left.

How many **apples** did his **horse** eat?

.... apples

2 marks

Score:

Summer Term: Workout 2

Warm up

1. Count **in steps of five** to fill in the **missing numbers**.

   45   50   65   ....

   2 marks

2. Work out these **divisions**.

   10 ÷ 2 = ...   60 ÷ 10 = ...

   2 marks

3. Colour in the shape with **no lines of symmetry**.

      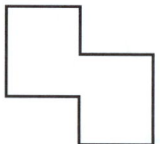  

   1 mark

4. Write **true** or **false** next to each **sentence**.

   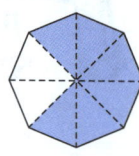 $\frac{3}{4}$ of the shape is shaded.   ....

   1 mark

   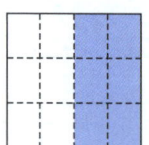 $\frac{1}{4}$ of the shape is shaded.   ....

   1 mark

5. Use the **pictures** to fill in the **missing numbers**.

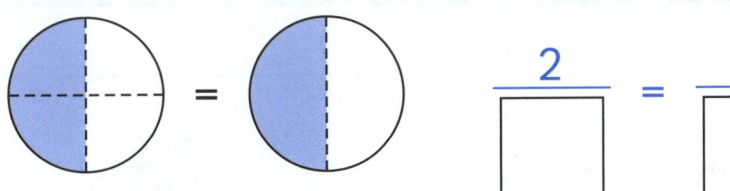

1 mark

6. A **big sweet** costs **27p** and a **small sweet** costs **16p**.
   How much do they **cost** in **total**?

.... p

1 mark

7. What is $\frac{1}{4}$ of **8 cm**?

.... cm

1 mark

8. A snail took part in **three** races.
   The **table** shows how long it took to finish each race.

Race	A	B	C
Time	5 hours	8 hours	7 hours

Did the snail take **more** or **less** than **one day**
to finish all three races? Show your working.

....

2 marks

Score:

Summer Term: Workout 3

Warm up

1. Write these numbers in **words**.

    85 ....

    1 mark

    100 ....

    1 mark

2. Work out these **subtractions**.

    27 − 10 = ...

    73 − 40 = ...

    2 marks

3. What **temperature** is shown on this **thermometer**?

 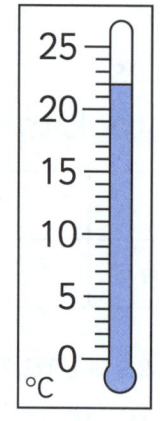

    ....°C

    1 mark

4. Circle the numbers with **two even digits**.

    18   25   32   44   56   62   77

    1 mark

5. Draw the next **two patterns** in this **sequence**.

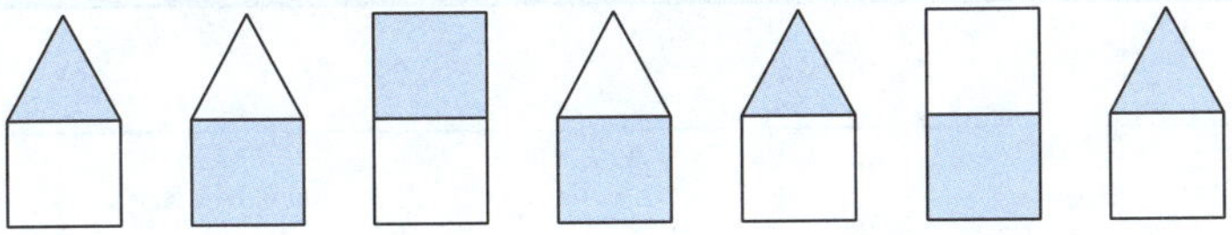

....

2 marks

6. Look at this picture.

The picture is **turned clockwise**.
Match the **pictures** to the **correct description**.

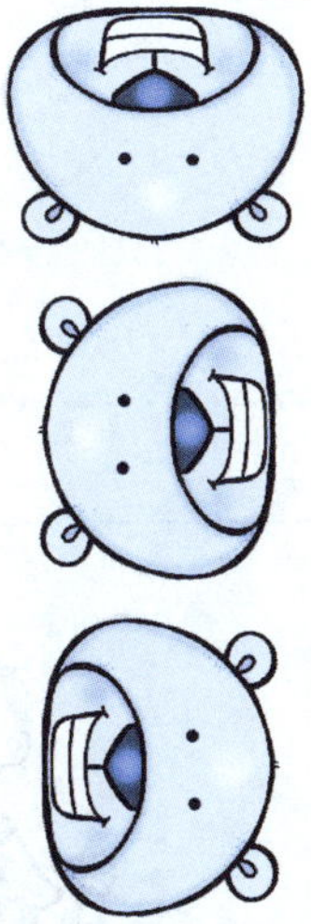

turned one right angle

turned two right angles

turned three right angles

2 marks

7. Karl has **£18**.

Lucy has **half** as much money as Karl.

How much money do they have **altogether**?

£........................

2 marks

Score:

Summer Term: Workout 4

Warm up

1. **Estimate** the numbers the **arrows** are pointing to.

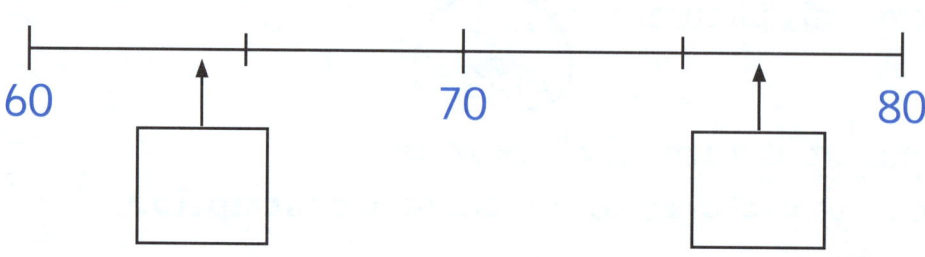

2 marks

2. Work out these **multiplications**.

   3 × 2 = ...   3 × 5 = ...

   2 marks

3. Put these **in order**. Start with the **largest**. Write your answers as **numbers**.

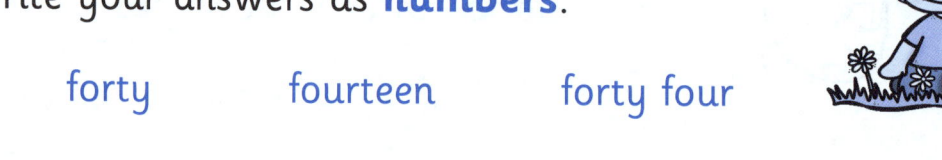

   ....
   largest   smallest

   2 marks

4. Fill in the **missing numbers**.

   There are .... minutes in an hour

   1 mark

   and .... hours in a day.

   1 mark

5. Draw **a line of symmetry** on this triangle.

 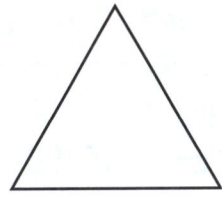

1 mark

6. **Two trees** are growing in a forest.

   The **oak** tree is **18 metres** tall.
   The **fir** tree is **14 metres taller**.

   How **tall** is the **fir tree**?

.... metres

1 mark

7. Nadia has a **code** for writing numbers.

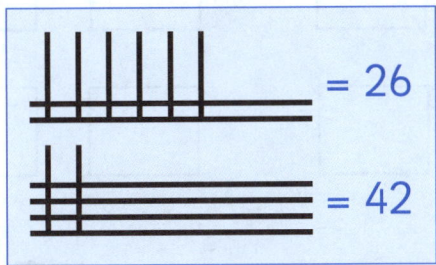 

Work out the **answer** to this calculation.
Give your answer as a **number**.

 = ...

2 marks

Score:

Summer Term: Workout 5

Warm up

1. Count **backwards** in **steps of 10** to fill in the **missing numbers**.

   100 .... 70 ....

   2 marks

2. Work out these **additions**.

   4 + 2 + 2 = ...   6 + 3 + 8 = ...

   2 marks

3. Make **four different** number sentences. **Only** use the numbers in the **box**.

   16   41   25

   ☐ + ☐ = ☐   ☐ + ☐ = ☐

   ☐ − ☐ = ☐   ☐ − ☐ = ☐

   2 marks

4. Carlos buys a drink for **44p**.

   He pays with **three 20p coins**.

   How much **change** does he get?

   ....p

   2 marks

5. This **block diagram** shows the number of times some **superheroes** have saved the day.

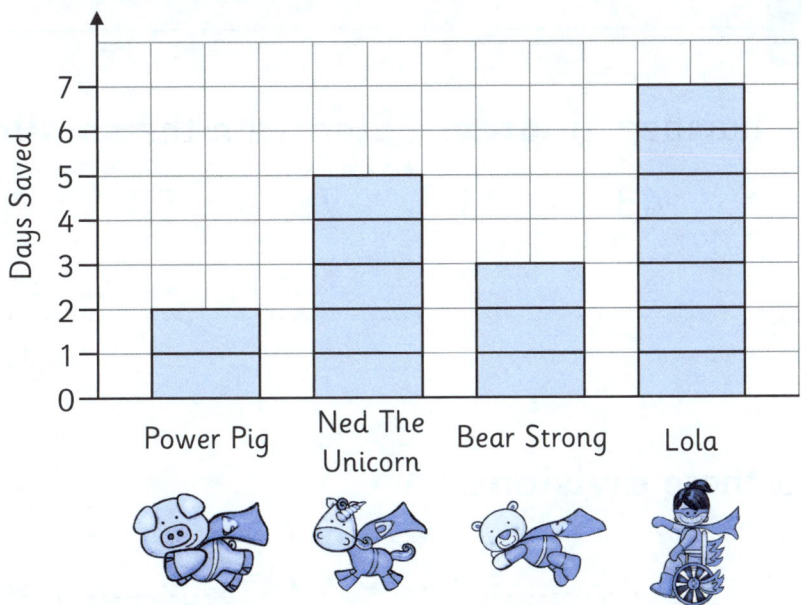

Which hero has saved the day **3 times**?

....
1 mark

Who has saved the day the **most times**?

....
1 mark

6. **Ten chairs** weigh **50 kg**.

Three tables weigh **30 kg**.

How much **more** does a **table** weigh than a **chair**?

.... kg
2 marks

Score:

Summer Term: Workout 6

Warm up

1. Put these numbers **in order**. Start with the **smallest**.

   31   43   11   78   50

   ....
   smallest   largest

   2 marks

2. Work out these **divisions**.

   20 ÷ 5 = ...   18 ÷ 2 = ...

   2 marks

3. James went to the **park**. He saw **7 giraffes**, **4 whales** and **6 gorillas**.

   How many **animals** did he see **in total**?

   .... animals

   1 mark

4. What **times** are shown on these **clocks**?

         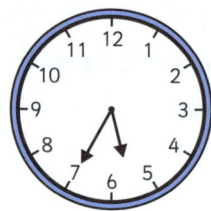

   ....

   2 marks

5. Fill in the **missing 2D shape** in this sentence.

   Each face on a cube is a ....

   1 mark

6. Join up the **pictures** to the right **fraction**.

   $\frac{1}{2}$ shaded

   $\frac{1}{4}$ shaded

   $\frac{1}{3}$ shaded

   $\frac{3}{4}$ shaded

   3 marks

7. Ali and Ben find these **coins** under their sofa. They **share** them **evenly**.

   How much do they **each** get?

   .... p

   1 mark

   Score:

Summer Term: Workout 7

Warm up

1. Count **backwards** in **steps of three** to fill in the **missing numbers**.

   21   18   9   ....

   2 marks

2. Work out these **subtractions**.

   56 – 3 = ...   91 – 9 = ...

   2 marks

3. **Cross out** (*X*) the **calculation** that gives a **different answer** to the others.

   5 + 5 + 5 + 5

   4 × 5

   4 + 4 + 4 + 4

   1 mark

4. Circle **four coins** that add up to **85p**.

   2 marks

5. How many **quarters** are the same as **one half**?
   Circle your answer.

            1   2   4   8

   1 mark

6. Sort these **shapes** into the correct part of the **table**.
   One has been done for you.

   A   B   C   D   E   F

Has a line of symmetry	Does not have a line of symmetry
A	

   3 marks

7. Louis thinks of a **number**.

   He says, "My number is **odd**. If you **add up** the **digits**, you get an **even** number."

   Which of these could be **Louis' number**?
   Circle your answer.

       22   23   32   33

   1 mark

   Score:

Summer Term: Workout 8

Warm up

1. **Cross out** (X) all of the **even numbers**.

   27   61   82   59   40   25   78

   2 marks

2. Join up the **three pairs** of numbers that **add up to 100**.

   20   10

   40   60

   90   80

   2 marks

3. Write **<** or **>** in each box.

   one metre ☐ one centimetre   *1 mark*

   one gram ☐ one kilogram   *1 mark*

   one litre ☐ one millilitre   *1 mark*

4. Fill in the **missing numbers**.

   12 × 5 = 60, so .... ÷ 5 = ...

   1 mark

5. Priya counted the **types of song** she listened to.

Song	Pop	Rock	Jazz
Tally	|||||	||||	||||||

   Which type of song did she listen to the **fewest** times?

   ....
   1 mark

   Priya says, "I listened to **14 songs** in total."
   Is she **right**? Show your working.

   ....
   1 mark

6. There are **28 people** on a **bus**.

   At the next stop, **22 people get on** the bus and **16 people get off** the bus.

   How many **people** are on the bus now? Show your working.

   .... people
   2 marks

   Score:

Summer Term: Workout 9

Warm up

1. Fill in the **missing numbers**.

   The number **94** has .... tens and .... ones.

   1 mark

2. Work out these **additions**.

   12 + 12 = ...

   44 + 22 = ...

   2 marks

3. Dennis has written these **number sentences**.

   Circle the number sentence that is **wrong**.

   19 < 31   42 > 26

   51 < 15   92 > 22

   1 mark

4. Circle **all** the **correct calculations**.

   3 × 5 = 15   15 ÷ 5 = 3   3 × 15 = 5

   3 ÷ 5 = 15   15 ÷ 3 = 5

   2 marks

5. Joe is counting **in steps**.
   Here are **some** of the
   numbers he says.

   What **number** is he counting in **steps** of?

   ....

   1 mark

6. A movie lasts for **1 hour** and **10 minutes**.

   How many **minutes** is this **in total**?

   .... minutes

   2 marks

7. Saki's squash comes in **cartons** and **bottles**.

   A **carton** holds **2 litres** of squash.
   A **bottle** holds the same amount as **3 cartons**.

   How much does a **bottle** hold?

   .... litres

   1 mark

8. Fill in the next **two boxes** in the **sequence**.

   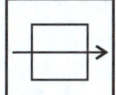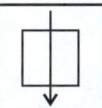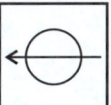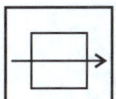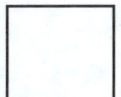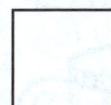

   2 marks

   Score:

Summer Term: Workout 10

Warm up

1. Fill in the **missing numbers** by counting **backwards** in steps of **two**.

   24 .... 18 ....

   2 marks

2. Work out these **multiplications**.

   10 × 10 = ...   7 × 5 = ...

   2 marks

3. Fill in the **missing number**.

   9 + ... + 7 = 20

   1 mark

4. Circle the **best estimate** for the **height** of:

   a house   6 metres   6 centimetres

1 mark

   a mug   10 metres   10 centimetres

1 mark

5. Fill in the **missing numbers**.

   A cube has .... edges,

   6 faces and .... vertices.

   1 mark

6. Work out:

   $\frac{1}{2}$ of 22 = ...

   $\frac{3}{4}$ of 12 = ...

   2 marks

7. A **rocket** is flying in space.

   The rocket moves **forward 3** squares.

   It then turns **one right angle anticlockwise**.

   Last, it moves **forward 2** squares.

   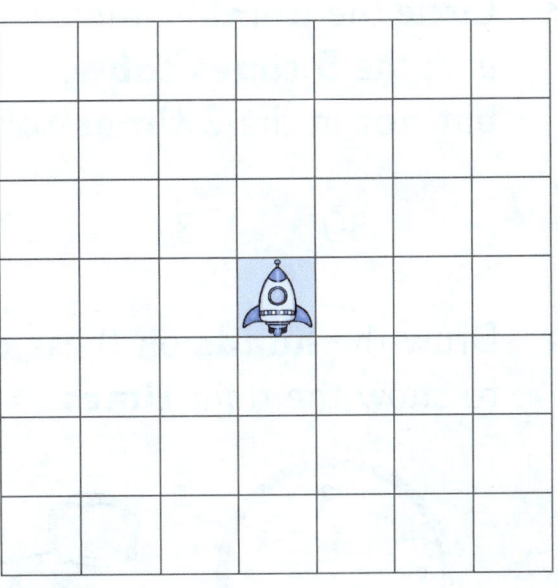

   Colour in the **squares** to show **where** the rocket goes.

   2 marks

   Score:

Summer Term: Workout 11

Warm up

1. Write these words as **numbers**.

   sixty three ....   fifty ....

   2 marks

2. Work out these **subtractions**.

   88 − 18 = ...

   31 − 29 = ...

   2 marks

3. Circle the **number** that is in the **5 times table**, but **not** in the **2 times table**.

   30   31   35   39   40

   1 mark

4. Draw the **hands** on these **clock faces** to show the right **times**.

   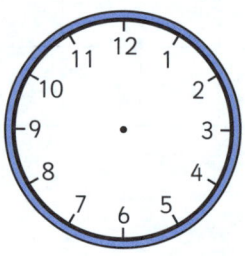
   25 past 7

   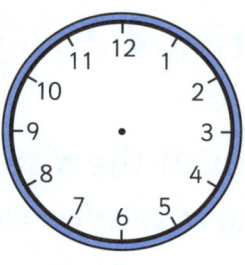
   quarter to 2

   2 marks

5. Barack sold **2 shark** shirts, **3 flower** shirts and **5 tree** shirts.

   Complete this **pictogram** showing the number of shirts he sold.

Shirt	Number Sold
Crab	△ △ △ △
Shark	
Flower	
Tree	

   Key:
   △ = 1 shirt

   2 marks

   How many **shirts** did he sell in **total**?

   .... shirts   *1 mark*

6. Look at these **scales**.

    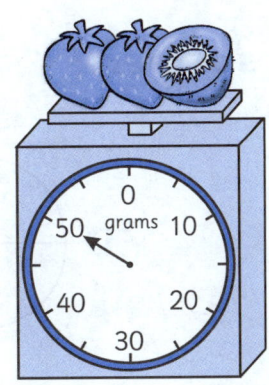

   Work out the **weight** of:

    .... grams   .... grams

   2 marks

   Score:

Summer Term: Workout 12

Warm up

1. These numbers go up by the **same amount** each time. Fill in the **missing numbers**.

   33   43   73   ....

   2 marks

2. Put these numbers **in order**. Start with the **largest**.

   46   84   68   66   48

   ....
   largest   smallest

   2 marks

3. Look at the **spinner**.

   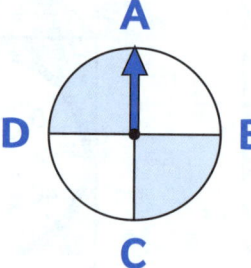

   What **letter** will the arrow **point to** if it turns:

   clockwise one right angle?   ....   *1 mark*

   anticlockwise three right angles?   ....   *1 mark*

4. Colour in the **hexagon**.

1 mark

5. Corey has read **45 stories** out of the **92 stories** in a **book**.

   How many **stories** does he have **left** to read?

   .... stories

   1 mark

6. Fill in the **missing fractions**.

   ☐/☐ of 8 is 2   ☐/☐ of 12 is 4

   2 marks

7. Evan paid for **3 sweets** using a **50p coin**.

   The **change** he got is **exactly** enough to buy **2 more sweets**.

   How much does **1 sweet** cost?

   .... p

   2 marks

   Score: ☐

Progress Chart

Fill in the progress chart after you finish each workout.

Put your scores in here to see how you've done. Each workout is out of 12 marks.

	Autumn Term	Spring Term	Summer Term
Workout 1			
Workout 2			
Workout 3			
Workout 4			
Workout 5			
Workout 6			
Workout 7			
Workout 8			
Workout 9			
Workout 10			
Workout 11			
Workout 12			

Answers

Autumn Term

Workout 1 — pages 2-3

1.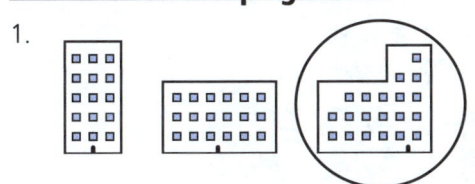
   1 mark

2. **twelve** 1 mark   **seventeen** 1 mark

3.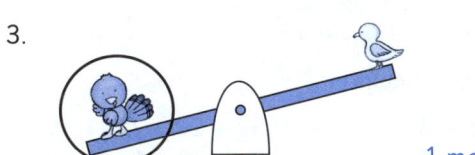
   1 mark

4. 4 × 2 = **8** 1 mark   3 × 5 = **15** 1 mark

5. **giraffe** ✓   candle ☐   doll ☐   1 mark

6. **half past 1** 1 mark

7. 6 add 12 equals **18** 1 mark
   18 subtract 7 equals **11** 1 mark

8. **a quarter turn anticlockwise** ✓
   a half turn clockwise ☐
   a three-quarter turn clockwise ✓
   a quarter turn clockwise ☐
   2 marks for both correct turns ticked only, otherwise 1 mark for one correct turn ticked

Workout 2 — pages 4-5

1.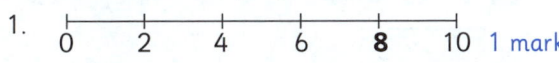
   1 mark

2. 3 **+** 4 = 7   4 = 5 − 1   1 mark
   10 − 8 = 2   9 = 4 **+** 5   1 mark

3.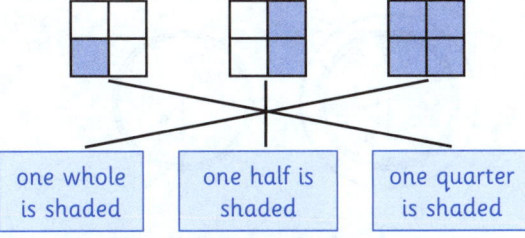
   2 marks for all three correct lines, otherwise 1 mark for any one correct line

4. 10 hours (**15 hours**) 1 hour   1 mark

5. **triangle** 1 mark   **rectangle** 1 mark

6. 14 add 6 equals **20**   1 mark
   19 subtract 3 equals **16**   1 mark

7. Each child gets **3 pencils**. 1 mark

8. The next number in the pattern is one less than the previous number. So the 5th is 96, the 6th is 95 and the 7th is **94**. 1 mark

Workout 3 — pages 6-7

1. 14   11   (**16**)   9   1 mark

2.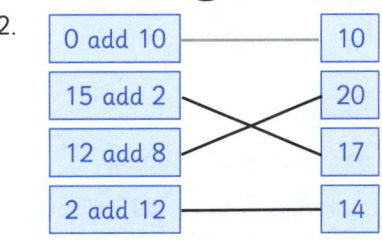
   2 marks for all three correct lines, otherwise 1 mark for any one correct line

3.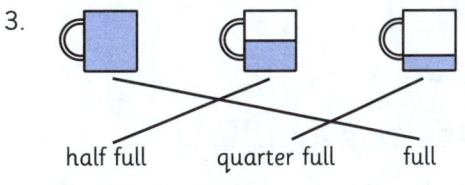
   2 marks for all three correct lines, otherwise 1 mark for any one correct line

4. **12** + 3 = 15 1 mark   3 = **11** − 8   1 mark

5. **Saturday** 1 mark

6. 10 15 20 25 30
   ☐ ✗ ☐ ✗ ☐   1 mark

7.
   1 mark for each correct answer

8. He needs 7 × 2 = **14 flags** in total   1 mark

Workout 4 — pages 8-9

1. 99 is one more than 100 ☐
   101 is one more than 100 ✓ 1 mark
2. 8 + 4 = **12** 1 mark   14 + 4 = **18** 1 mark
3. 65 has a **6** in the tens place
   and a **5** in the ones place. 1 mark
4. E.g.

   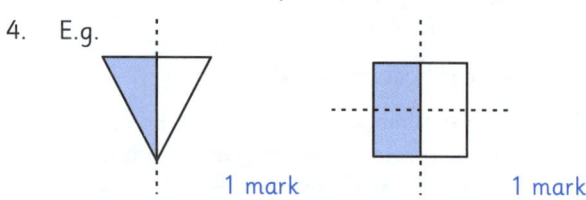

   1 mark   1 mark

5.

   6 kg   10 kg   2 kg
   ☐   ☐   ✓   1 mark

6. **96** 1 mark
   seventy six 1 mark
7. 70 > 47 1 mark   22 < 29 1 mark
8. When both hands point to 12, it is 12 o'clock.
   So the time now must be 1 o'clock:

   1 mark

Workout 5 — pages 10-11

1. **19** 1 mark
2. 1 = 5 − 4 1 mark   7 + 3 = 10 1 mark
3. **8 litres** 1 mark
4.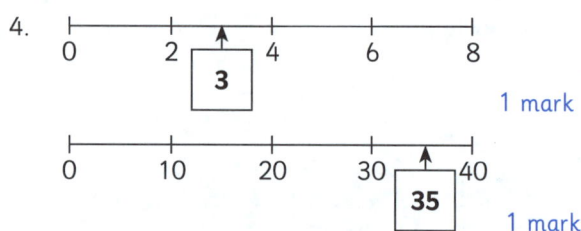

   1 mark

   1 mark

5. 17, 27, 37, **47** 1 mark
6. 10 ÷ 2 = **5** 1 mark
7. 3 tens = **30** 1 mark
   2 tens and 6 ones = **26** 1 mark

8. One more than 15 is 16.
   Half of 16 is 8, so her sum is **8 + 8 = 16**.
   1 mark for finding one more than 15,
   1 mark for finding half of their answer

Workout 6 — pages 12-13

1. **12 − 2 = 10** 1 mark
2. **6 × 2 = 12** 1 mark
   4 × 5 = 20 1 mark
3.

   1 mark

4. 8 + 3 + 6 = **17** 1 mark
5. There are **7** days in a week. 1 mark
6. 31 + 8 = **39** 1 mark   52 + 20 = **72** 1 mark
   48 − 6 = **42** 1 mark   97 − 30 = **67** 1 mark
7.

   1 mark

8. E.g. The numbers in the circles go up in tens.
   So the number in the next circle would be
   20 + 10 = **30**. 1 mark

Workout 7 — pages 14-15

1.

   1 mark

2. 3 + 8 = **11** 1 mark   14 − 7 = **7** 1 mark
3. **8 + 12 = 20** 1 mark
   12 + 8 = 20 1 mark
4. E.g.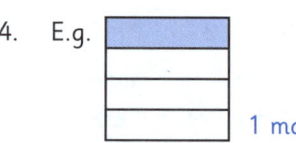

   1 mark

5.

   1 mark

6. 30 + 70 = 100 1 mark
   20 + **80** = 100 1 mark
7. 10p + 10p = **20p** 1 mark
   20p + 5p + 1p = **26p** 1 mark
8. **Glass C** 1 mark
   (Glass A is less than a quarter full.
   Glass B is more than half full.)

Workout 8 — pages 16-17

1. 8, **6**, **4**, 2 1 mark
2.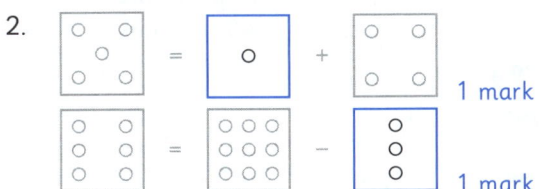
   1 mark
   1 mark
3. The toothbrush is **10** blocks long. 1 mark
4. 14 + 23 = **37** 1 mark   38 − 16 = **22** 1 mark
5.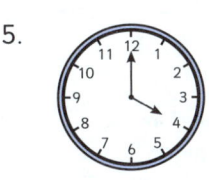
   1 mark   1 mark
6. 27 + 12 = **39** 1 mark   66 − 34 = **32** 1 mark
7. 3 × **10** = **30** 1 mark
8. 25 − 10 = 15, 15 − 3 = 12
   So 25 − 13 = **12 seeds** 1 mark

Workout 9 — pages 18-19

1. **20** 1 mark
2. 10 + 5 = **15** 1 mark
   8 + 10 = **18** 1 mark
3.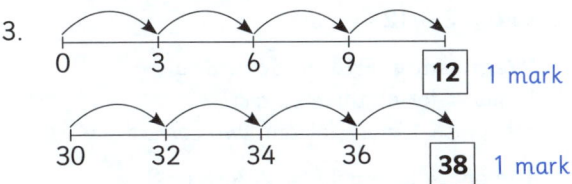
   1 mark
   1 mark
4. 7 ㉒ 31 ㉞ 43
   1 mark for each correct answer
5.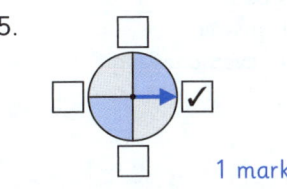
   1 mark

6. One **half** of the shape is shaded. 1 mark
7. 2 × 10 = **20** 1 mark   25 ÷ 5 = 5 1 mark
8. One less than 19 is 18,
   so her second throw was **18 m**. 1 mark

Workout 10 — pages 20-21

1.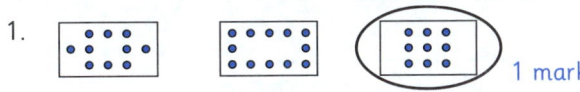
   1 mark
2.
   1 mark for each correct answer
3. 50, **40**, **30**, 20, 10
   2 marks for all four correct,
   otherwise 1 mark for any two correct
4. E.g.
   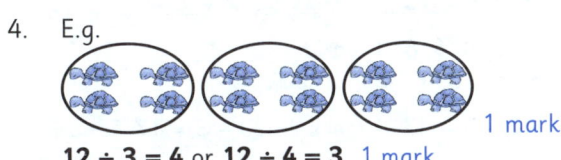
   1 mark
   12 ÷ 3 = 4 or **12 ÷ 4 = 3** 1 mark
5. 6 × 10 = 10 × **6** 1 mark
6.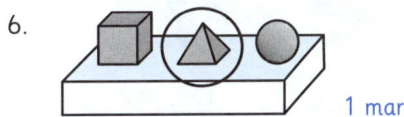
   1 mark
7. 4 × 5 = 20 1 mark   6 = 30 ÷ 5 1 mark
8. **Jordan** has the quickest time,
   so he won the race. 1 mark

Workout 11 — pages 22-23

1.
   1 mark
2. 8 ÷ 2 = **4** 1 mark   10 ÷ 5 = **2** 1 mark
3. 1p (100p) 10p (£1) £10
   1 mark for each correct answer
4. (ruler with cross at 5 cm)
   1 mark for a cross at 5 cm (allow 4.9-5.1 cm)
5.
   1 mark
   1 mark

6.
```
□ − 7 = 13        0
20 − □ = 20       10
20 − □ = 10       19
20 − 1 = □        20
```
3 marks for all four correct lines,
otherwise 2 marks for any two correct lines
or 1 mark for any one correct line

7. She has 4 − 3 = 1 slice left.
1 of 4 equal slices is the same as **one quarter**.
1 mark

Workout 12 — pages 24-25

1. 0, 2, 4, **6**, **8**   1 mark
   0, 5, 10, 15, **20**   1 mark

2. 16 − 3 = **13**   1 mark   20 − 3 = **17**   1 mark

3. 20 − 15 = 5, so he gets a 5p coin.

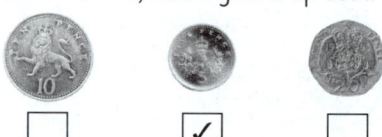
1 mark

4. 6 × 2 = **12**   1 mark   4 × 5 = **20**   1 mark

5. 25 + 40 = **65p**   1 mark
   40 − 20 = 20
   20 − 5 = **15p**   1 mark

6. She must pay with two 20p coins and
   one 10p coin to get no change:

2 marks for three correct coins circled, otherwise
1 mark for any two correct coins circled

7. If yesterday was Tuesday, today is Wednesday
   and tomorrow is Thursday.
   So Felix's birthday is on **Thursday**.   1 mark

Spring Term

Workout 1 — pages 26-27

1. 57, 58, **59**, **60**, 61, **62**
   2 marks for all three correct numbers,
   otherwise 1 mark for any two correct numbers

2. 6 ⑨ ⑮ 18 22 28 50 ㊼
   2 marks for all three correct numbers only,
   otherwise 1 mark for any two correct numbers

3. 2p + 2p + 1p + 1p + 1p = **7p**   1 mark
   20p + 10p + 10p + 5p = **45p**   1 mark

4. **79 + 9**   1 mark

5. **86** − 75 = 11   1 mark

6. E.g.

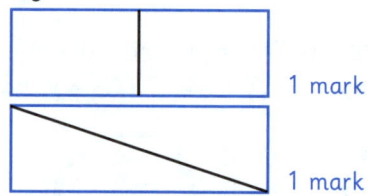
1 mark

1 mark

7. 15 + 20 = 35 bananas in total   1 mark
   35 − 4 = **31 bananas** left   1 mark

Workout 2 — pages 28-29

1. 40 + 20 = **60**   1 mark
   55 − 30 = **25**   1 mark

2. **5**   1 mark   **23**   1 mark

3. **Sphere**   1 mark

4. 10 × 4 = **40 legs**   1 mark

5. 7 × 5 = 35, so Nora is **7 years old**   1 mark

6. There are six 2s added together,
   so **6 × 2 = 12**   1 mark

7. **Wednesday**, **Friday**, **Saturday**
   2 marks for all three correct,
   otherwise 1 mark for any two correct

8. The ones digit could be 2, 4, 6 or 8.
   Three times 4, 6 or 8 makes a two-digit number,
   so the tens digit must be 2 × 3 = 6.
   So Jasmine's number is **62**.
   2 marks for the correct answer,
   otherwise 1 mark for an even ones digit

Workout 3 — pages 30-31

1. **nineteen** 1 mark   **eleven** 1 mark
2. 87, 77, **67**, **57**, 47 1 mark
3. E.g.

    1 mark

    1 mark

4. a train   cm ☐   **m** ✓ 1 mark
   a carrot **cm** ✓ m ☐ 1 mark

5. 2   5   8   **(10)**   15
   16 **(20)** 22 25 **(30)**

   2 marks for all three correct numbers only, otherwise 1 mark for any two correct numbers

6. The ant's length **<** The caterpillar's length 1 mark

7. Left box: 20 + 20 + 10 + 10 + 10 = 70p
   Right box: 5 + 5 = 10p
   70 − 10 = 60p, so:

   [50p] [10p]

   1 mark for working out the remaining total,
   1 mark for two coins that add up to their total

Workout 4 — pages 32-33

1. 11 + 3 = **14** 1 mark   8 + 9 = **17** 1 mark
2. The number 37 has **3** tens and **7** ones. 1 mark
3. Reading: top /**(middle)**/ bottom book 1 mark
   Maths: **(top)**/ middle / bottom book 1 mark
4. 25 grams   **(25 kilograms)** 1 mark
   (10 grams)   10 kilograms 1 mark
5. 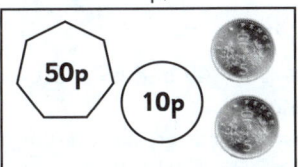   2 × 5   10 × 10   **(4 × 5)**
   (10 × 2)   5 × 2   4 × 10   4 × 2
   5 × 10   **(2 × 10)**   12 × 5

   2 marks for all three correct answers only, otherwise 1 mark for any two correct answers

6. The mass of the egg **>** 45 grams 1 mark

7. Jayden has 6 + 2 = 8 points 1 mark
   So they have 6 + 8 + 3 = **17 points** altogether 1 mark

Workout 5 — pages 34-35

1. 5, 10, 15, **20**, 25 1 mark
2. 42 + 10 = **52** 1 mark   77 − 60 = **17** 1 mark
3. E.g.

   1 mark   1 mark

4. 4 × 5 = 20   20 ÷ 5 = 4   ~~4 ÷ 20 = 5~~
   ~~5 ÷ 20 = 4~~   5 × 4 = 20   20 ÷ 4 = 5

   1 mark for each correct answer

5. 10 ml **<** 1 litre 1 mark

6. **D**, **B**, **C**, **A**
   2 marks for all jugs in the correct order, otherwise
   1 mark for any three jugs in the correct order
   Jug **C** 1 mark

7. Maths Club was on yesterday, so it must be Tuesday, Thursday or Saturday. It isn't on tomorrow, so it must be **Saturday**. 1 mark

Workout 6 — pages 36-37

1. 3 × 6 = **18** 1 mark
2. 58 − 4 = **54** 1 mark   81 − 10 = **71** 1 mark
3. 3 4 **(5)** 6 7 8 1 mark
4.

Has 6 sides	Does not have 6 sides
B, D	**A, C, E**

   2 marks for all four shapes correctly sorted, otherwise 1 mark for two shapes correctly sorted

5. 34 + 55 = **89** 1 mark   48 + 34 = **82** 1 mark

6. E.g.

   1 mark

7. 1 mark

8. Abbie says: 0, 5, 10, 15, 20, 25...
   Kaine says: 0, 3, 6, 9, 12, 15, 18...
   So the first number they both say is **15**
   2 marks for the correct answer,
   otherwise 1 mark for a correct method

Workout 7 — pages 38-39

1. **Tigers** 1 mark
2. **twenty six** 1 mark   **seventy three** 1 mark
3. 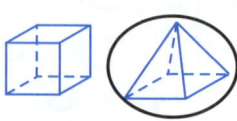 1 mark
4.  1 mark
5. **48, 41, 34, 32**
   2 marks for all numbers in the correct order,
   otherwise 1 mark for any three numbers in the correct order
6.
Faces	Edges	Vertices
5	9	6

   1 mark for each correct column
   Two of the faces are triangles 1 mark
7. Pressing the button four times makes the arrow do a whole turn, and two times makes it do a half turn. So, for two and a half turns, you need to press the button 4 + 4 + 2 = **10 times**
   2 marks for the correct answer,
   otherwise 1 mark for showing correct number of button presses for a whole or a half turn

Workout 8 — pages 40-41

1.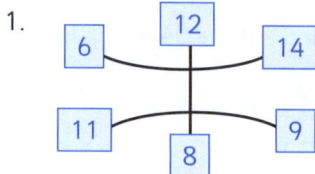
   2 marks for all three correct lines,
   otherwise 1 mark for any one correct line
2. 15, **18**, **21**, **24**, 27
   2 marks for all three correct numbers,
   otherwise 1 mark for any two correct numbers

3. 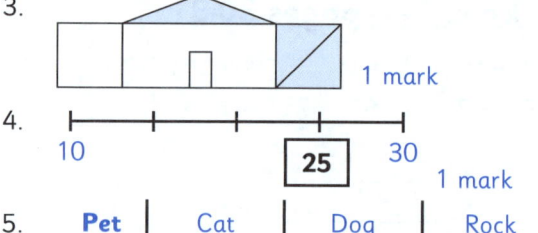 1 mark
4. 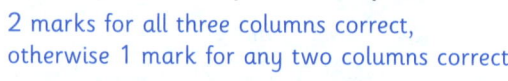 1 mark
5.
Pet	Cat	Dog	Rock
Tally	||||		||||	||

   2 marks for all three columns correct,
   otherwise 1 mark for any two columns correct
   Cat 1 mark   4 − 2 = **2 people** 1 mark
6. 5 pumpkins weigh 6 × 5 = 30 kilograms.
   3 watermelons weigh 8 × 3 = 24 kilograms.
   So, weight of 5 pumpkins **>** weight of 3 watermelons.
   1 mark for at least one correct calculation,
   1 mark for the correct answer

Workout 9 — pages 42-43

1. 5 + **6** = 11 1 mark   15 − **7** = 8 1 mark
2. 4 × 5 = **20** 1 mark   7 × 2 = **14** 1 mark
3. **half past 1** 1 mark
4. **No**, because 19 + 30 = 49 and 69 − 30 = 39, so they are not equal.
   1 mark for at least one correct calculation,
   1 mark for the correct answer
5.  1 mark
   Caleb 1 mark
   3 + 2 + 5 + 2 = **12 goals** 1 mark
6. **50p**, **20p** and **5p** 1 mark
   50p, **10p**, **10p** and **5p** 1 mark

Workout 10 — pages 44-45

1. 16, **14**, **12**, 10, 8, **6**
   2 marks for all three correct numbers,
   otherwise 1 mark for any two correct numbers
2. 7 + 3 + 2 = **12** 1 mark
   6 + 4 + 8 = **18** 1 mark

3.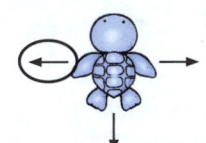
   1 mark

4. 8 + 2 is the same as 2 + 8 ✓
   8 − 2 is the same as 2 − 8 ☐
   8 × 2 is the same as 2 × 8 ✓
   8 ÷ 2 is the same as 2 ÷ 8 ☐
   1 mark for each correct answer

5. **8 loaves**, **4 rolls** and **6 cakes**
   2 marks for all three correct numbers,
   otherwise 1 mark for any two correct numbers
   4 × 10 = **40p**   1 mark

6. 6**5** + 32 = 97   1 mark
   6**2** + 35 = 97   1 mark

Workout 11 — pages 46-47

1. 12 ÷ 4 = **3**   1 mark   12 ÷ 3 = **4**   1 mark
2. 3 4 ⑥ 7 11 ⑭ 15 19   1 mark
3. 36 + 11 = **47**   1 mark   25 + 25 = **50**   1 mark
4.  1 mark    1 mark
5.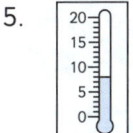
   1 mark
   The hottest country is Egypt: **20 °C**   1 mark
   Italy is 13 °C, so it is 13 − 8
   = **5 °C** warmer than the UK.   1 mark
6. Flora has 7 × 3 = 21 apples
   Monty has 4 × 5 = 20 apples
   So **Flora** has more apples.
   1 mark for at least one correct calculation,
   1 mark for the correct answer

Workout 12 — pages 48-49

1. 17 − 7 = **10**   1 mark   13 − 8 = **5**   1 mark
2. 21 **<** 67   54 **=** 54   93 **>** 88
   2 marks for all three correct answers,
   otherwise 1 mark for any two correct answers

3.    1 mark

4. Number of minutes in an hour — 7
   Number of hours in a day — 24
   Number of days in a week — 60
   (lines cross: minutes→60, hours→24, days→7)
   2 marks for all three correct lines,
   otherwise 1 mark for any one correct line

5. Zack's ride lasted for 60 minutes,
   so **Maisie** had the longest ride.   1 mark

6. 6 ÷ 2 = 3   9 × 2 = 18   1 mark

7. 24 + 3 = 30 − **3**   1 mark

8. The highest value coins less than £1
   that are shaped like circles are 10p and 5p.
   The highest value coin less than £1
   that isn't shaped like a circle is 50p.
   So the largest amount Saffron could have
   is 50p + 10p + 5p = **65p**
   2 marks for the correct answer,
   otherwise 1 mark for a correct method

Summer Term

Workout 1 — pages 50-51

1. The number **72** has 7 tens and 2 ones.   1 mark
2. 83 + 5 = **88**   1 mark   48 + 7 = **55**   1 mark
3. E.g.
   1 mark
   18 ÷ 3 = **6**   1 mark
4. Weight of the pencil < Weight of the sharpener
   1 mark
5. circle   ⟨rectangle⟩   cube   triangle
   pyramid   ⟨square⟩   sphere
   1 mark for each correct answer
6. ½ of 10 is 5   1 mark   ⅓ of 9 is 3   1 mark
7. 30 − 8 = 22   1 mark
   22 − 19 = 3, so the horse ate **3 apples**   1 mark

Workout 2 — pages 52-53

1. 45, 50, **55**, **60**, 65, **70**
   2 marks for all three correct numbers,
   otherwise 1 mark for any two correct numbers
2. 10 ÷ 2 = **5**   1 mark   60 ÷ 10 = **6**   1 mark
3. [shapes with pentagon shaded]   1 mark
4. **True**   1 mark   **False**   1 mark
5. $\frac{2}{4} = \frac{1}{2}$ 1 mark
6. 27p + 16p = **43p**   1 mark
7. **2 cm**   1 mark
8. 5 + 8 + 7 = 20 hours   1 mark
   1 day = 24 hours, so the snail took
   less than 1 day to finish the races.   1 mark

Workout 3 — pages 54-55

1. **eighty five**   1 mark   **one hundred**   1 mark
2. 27 − 10 = **17**   1 mark   73 − 40 = **33**   1 mark
3. **22 °C**   1 mark
4. 18   25   32   (**44**)   56   (**62**)   77   1 mark
5. [pattern of shapes]
   1 mark for each correct pattern
6.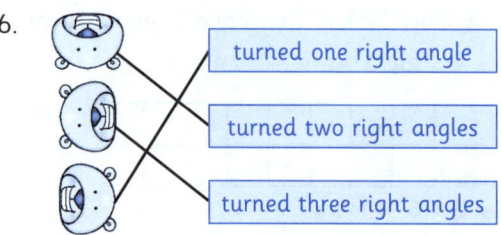
   2 marks for all three correct lines,
   otherwise 1 mark for any one correct line
7. Lucy has £18 ÷ 2 = £9   1 mark
   So together they have £18 + £9 = **£27**   1 mark

Workout 4 — pages 56-57

1.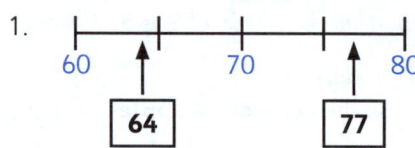
   1 mark for each correct number

2. 3 × 2 = **6**   1 mark   3 × 5 = **15**   1 mark
3. **44**, **40**, **14**
   1 mark for all three written as numbers
   correctly, 1 mark for the correct order
4. There are **60** minutes in an hour   1 mark
   and **24** hours in a day.   1 mark
5. E.g. [triangle with dashed line of symmetry]   1 mark
6. 18 + 14 = **32 metres**   1 mark
7. The codes mean 37 and 14,
   so the calculation is 37 − 14 = **23**
   2 marks for the correct answer,
   otherwise 1 mark for at least one code
   correctly converted to a number

Workout 5 — pages 58-59

1. 100, **90**, **80**, 70, **60**
   2 marks for all three correct numbers,
   otherwise 1 mark for any two correct numbers
2. 4 + 2 + 2 = **8**   1 mark   6 + 3 + 8 = **17**   1 mark
3. **16 + 25 = 41**   **25 + 16 = 41**   1 mark
   41 − 16 = 25   **41 − 25 = 16**   1 mark
4. 20p + 20p + 20p = 60p   1 mark
   60p − 44p = **16p**   1 mark
5. **Bear Strong**   1 mark
   Lola   1 mark
6. One chair weighs 50 ÷ 10 = 5 kg
   One table weighs 30 ÷ 3 = 10 kg
   So a table weighs 10 − 5 = **5 kg** more
   1 mark for at least one correct division,
   1 mark for the correct answer

Workout 6 — pages 60-61

1. **11**, **31**, **43**, **50**, **78**
   2 marks for all numbers in the correct order,
   otherwise 1 mark for any four numbers
   in the correct order
2. 20 ÷ 5 = **4**   1 mark   18 ÷ 2 = **9**   1 mark
3. 7 + 4 + 6 = **17 animals**   1 mark
4. **10 past 11**   1 mark
   25 to 6 or **35 past 5**   1 mark

Answers

5. Each face on a cube is a **square** 1 mark

6.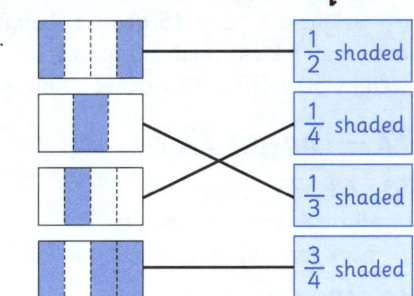

   3 marks for all four correct lines,
   otherwise 2 marks for any two correct lines
   or 1 mark for any one correct line

7. There are two 5p coins, two 10p coins
   and two 20p coins. So they each get
   5p + 10p + 20p = **35p** 1 mark

Workout 7 — pages 62-63

1. 21, 18, **15**, **12**, 9, **6**
   2 marks for all three correct numbers,
   otherwise 1 mark for any two correct numbers

2. 56 – 3 = **53** 1 mark   91 – 9 = **82** 1 mark

3. 5 + 5 + 5 + 5   4 × 5   ~~4 + 4 + 4 + 4~~ 1 mark

4.

   2 marks for all four correct coins circled, otherwise
   1 mark for at least three correct coins circled

5. 1 (**2**) 4 8 1 mark

6.

Has a line of symmetry	Does not have a line of symmetry
A, C, F	B, D, E

   3 marks for all five shapes correctly sorted,
   otherwise 2 marks for four shapes correctly
   sorted or 1 mark for two shapes correctly sorted

7. 22 and 32 are even, so they cannot be Louis'
   number. 2 + 3 = 5 is odd, but 3 + 3 is even,
   so **33** must be Louis' number. 1 mark

Workout 8 — pages 64-65

1. 27 61 ~~82~~ 59 ~~40~~ 25 ~~78~~
   2 marks for all three correct answers only,
   otherwise 1 mark for any two correct answers

2.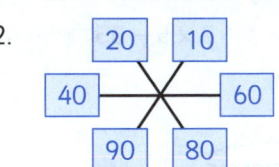

   2 marks for all three correct lines,
   otherwise 1 mark for any one correct line

3. One metre **>** one centimetre 1 mark
   One gram **<** one kilogram 1 mark
   One litre **>** one millilitre 1 mark

4. 12 × 5 = 60, so **60** ÷ 5 = **12** 1 mark

5. **Rock** 1 mark
   No, because 5 + 4 + 6 = 15 songs. 1 mark

6. 28 + 22 = 50
   50 – 16 = **34 people**
   2 marks for the correct answer,
   otherwise 1 mark for a correct method

Workout 9 — pages 66-67

1. The number 94 has **9** tens and **4** ones. 1 mark

2. 12 + 12 = **24** 1 mark   44 + 22 = **66** 1 mark

3. **51 < 15** 1 mark

4. (3 × 5 = 15)   (15 ÷ 5 = 3)   3 × 15 = 5
        3 ÷ 5 = 15   (15 ÷ 3 = 5)

   2 marks for all three correct calculations
   circled, otherwise 1 mark for any two correct
   calculations circled

5. E.g. 12 + 3 = 15, 15 + 3 = 18
   So Joe is counting in steps of **3** 1 mark

6. 1 hour = 60 minutes 1 mark
   60 + 10 = **70 minutes** 1 mark

7. 3 × 2 = **6 litres** 1 mark

8.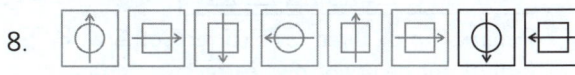

   1 mark for each correct box

Workout 10 — pages 68-69

1. 24, **22**, **20**, 18, **16**
   2 marks for all three correct numbers,
   otherwise 1 mark for any two correct numbers

2. 10 × 10 = **100** 1 mark   7 × 5 = **35** 1 mark

3. 9 + **4** + 7 = 20 1 mark

4. (**6 metres**) 6 centimetres   1 mark
   10 metres (**10 centimetres**) 1 mark

5. A cube has **12** edges, 6 faces and **8** vertices.
   1 mark

6. $\frac{1}{2}$ of 22 = **11** 1 mark $\frac{3}{4}$ of 12 = **9** 1 mark

7.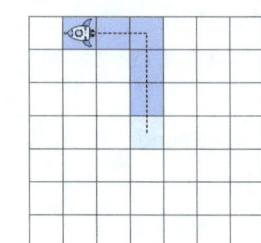
   2 marks for all correct squares shaded, otherwise
   1 mark for any two correct squares shaded

Workout 11 — pages 70-71

1. **63** 1 mark   **50** 1 mark

2. 88 − 18 = **70** 1 mark   31 − 29 = **2** 1 mark

3. 30   31   (**35**)   39   40   1 mark

4.  1 mark    1 mark

5.
Shirt	Number Sold
Crab	△△△△
Shark	△△
Flower	△△△
Tree	△△△△△

   2 marks for all three rows correct, otherwise
   1 mark for any two rows correct

   14 shirts 1 mark

Workout 12 — pages 72-73

1. 33, 43, **53**, **63**, 73, **83**
   2 marks for all three correct numbers,
   otherwise 1 mark for any two correct numbers

2. **84**, **68**, **66**, **48**, **46**
   2 marks for all numbers in the correct order,
   otherwise 1 mark for any four numbers
   in the correct order

3. **B** 1 mark   **B** 1 mark

4.    1 mark

5. 92 − 45 = **47 stories** 1 mark

6. $\frac{1}{4}$ of 8 is 2 1 mark $\frac{1}{3}$ of 12 is 4 1 mark

7. 50p is exactly enough to buy 3 + 2 = 5 sweets
   So one sweet costs 50 ÷ 5 = **10p**
   2 marks for the correct answer,
   otherwise 1 mark for a correct method

6. 2 strawberries weigh 30 grams, so
   1 strawberry weighs 30 ÷ 2 = **15 grams** 1 mark
   2 strawberries and 1 kiwi weigh 50 grams,
   so 1 kiwi weighs 50 − 30 = **20 grams** 1 mark